Letters Letters Everywhere

LEARNING

Uppercase and Lowercase LETTERS

A letter a week for 26-weeks daily workbook

By Heather Thomas

SpongyLittleMinds

No part of this book may be used, reproduced or transmitted in any form or by any means whatsoever, electronic or mechanical, including photocopying and recording, or by any information storage or retrieval system without prior written permission of the publisher/copyright owner.
Address requests for permissions to:
P.O. Box 3676
Nampa, ID. 83653
Or
info@spongylittleminds.com
Please include a phone number or e-mail address when contacting us.

Copyright © 2016 Saltiness Enterprises LLC
All rights reserved.

Acknowledgements

Thank you to my children, loved ones, and dearest friends, who have always believed in me and has always been there for me no matter what. And to my two youngest who out of the blue, in the same week, but two completely separate occasions, each said to me, "mommy, you need to finish your book". I finally did it! And last, but most definitely the greatest, to God for giving me the drive and persistence to push through and see it to the finish, all things come from you. Thank You!

Heather Thomas

Table of Contents

Preface

Free Stuff

Before Getting Started

Letter A Week 1

Days 1-4

Letter B Week 2

Days 5-8

Letter C Week 3

Days 9-12

Letter D Week 4

Days 13-16

Letter E Week 5

Days 17-20

Letter F Week 6

Days 21-24

Letter G Week 7

Days 25-29

Letter H Week 8

Days 29-32

Letter I Week 9

Days 33-36

Letter J Week 10

Days 37-40

Letter K Week 11

Days 41-44

Letter L Week 12

Days 45-48

Letter M Week 13

Days 49-52

Letter N Week 14

Days 53-56

Letter O Week 15

Days 57-60

Letter P Week 16

Days 61-64

Letter Q Week 17

Days 65-68

Letter R Week 18

Days 69-72

Letter S Week 19

Days 73-76

Letter T Week 20

Days 77-80

Letter U Week 21

Days 81-84

Letter V Week 22

Days 85-88

Letter W Week 23

Days 89-92

Letter X Week 24

Days 93-96

Letter Y Week 25

Days 97-100

Letter Z Week 26

Days 101-104

PREFACE

When I started putting this together for my two youngest children at home, my goal was for it to be a springboard into, "A Parents Guide to Teaching Reading" by Jessie Wise and Sara Buffington. My second goal was for it to be fairly simple and fun. My third goal was for it to be done without picture memory and sounds involved in order for them to truly master the letters at an early age.

My two youngest children had older siblings to compete with for time and learning materials. The four oldest had their workbooks and schooling that they were devouring everyday with enthusiasm and excitement. The two youngest wanted the same. I would look for workbooks that was just the letters, no extras, and I couldn't find any. There was always something that didn't fit with what I was trying to accomplish, either by using color, pictures, sounds, or only one worksheet per letter. So I made due and would improvise.

It seemed there was never enough worksheets. My children always wanted more. I was trying to build my own curriculum for them that would be systematic; making it easy for me to follow as a busy parent, and for them to anticipate the lessons. I built it as we went along and it worked. Not only were they grasping, fully retaining, and mastering the lessons, but they were also enjoying it, always wanting more. And I watched their dexterity, thinking, writing, and memory skills very quickly grow and improve. At three years old and up they were known to sometimes make a letter out of something they were eating or playing with. And I would even hear them shout out letters they would see when we were running errands in town. That's when I was very pleased. It was great!

I didn't have a lot of time. Our family was going through a transition, and I was trying to work through some college courses as well. Eventually I went into working part-time. We needed something consistent and basic that would fit our lifestyle at the time, yet give the children a solid foundation for routine, retention, recall, and their potential to grow and learn. I had become inspired to build my own letters workbook; which you see here today, that would fit the need of the curriculum I was building and saw working with my own children.

Not only did I use it with my children, but also had the opportunity to use it in a once-a-week small classroom setting (a homeschool co-op) as well. It was a little more challenging in a classroom setting, but I still saw a progression of improvement and success with the children's dexterity, thinking and memory skills, all with the parents help and involvement. It was very rewarding.

I hope that this book and SpongyLittleMinds.com will be of great value to you and your child, have fun!

Heather Thomas

This workbook works well for pre-school, kindergarten, or in a daycare setting. For homeschoolers it works well as a unit study or classical approach. It prepares your child for reading and so much more. If you have any questions in how to use this book in the different settings, or you simply don't know what any of this means, you can make contact through

www.spongylittleminds.com

I encourage and greatly appreciate your feedback! Please let me know how this book works for you!

FREE STUFF

VISIT OUR SITE TO LEARN MORE ABOUT FREE COMPANION PRINTOUTS AVAILABLE TO USE ALONG WITH THIS WORKBOOK!

Would you like to know more about:

⇒ a simple and affordable whole school year curriculum with a schedule, that is designed to go along with this workbook for the busy, overwhelmed, or unsure parent in mind

⇒ how you can start teaching your child early

⇒ homeschooling

⇒ the parent or teacher resources we have available

⇒ what we do and how we got started

⇒ any questions or feedback

We are here for you!

Visit www.SpongyLittleMinds.com.

And if you like this workbook we'd greatly enjoy the feedback, leave us a comment.

Before Getting Started - To the Parent

Before proceeding with this workbook I want to make you aware of something in order for you to hopefully understand the reason and goal behind this workbook and its curriculum, and to be able to use it correctly:

I do not, nor do you need to, make an emphasis on the sound of the letters at this time, it is not the focus of this workbook or the curriculum. We do not want to over load the child and they will be learning it when they start learning to read. We want to keep everything consistent, in order and making sense. To round it off, very focused and simple for the child and the parent. Right now the emphasis is on what the letter looks like, how to write it, the name, and the pairs of letters. That is really a lot in itself if you really want them to know, understand, and remember what they're learning. You want it all to sink in, thus your child is soaking it up. It's a matter of your child learning it concretely so they can be a master at what they're learning, which develops their self-esteem, confidence, memory muscles, and strengthens their brain power all at the same time.

Also, I do not use pictures to relate to the letters, so that they won't be distracted or hindered. They still have fun and enjoy it! This is what is stated in "The Well Trained Mind" by Susan Wise Bauer and Jesse Wise pg. 35; "*Sorting through charts and songs and trying to follow a program with lots of aids make teaching more complicated than it needs to be. Second, all those reinforcements and aids create extra mental steps for the learner. If you're teaching a child to sing the song "A is for apple, b is for bear, ...," you're teaching her to see an a, think "apple," and then think the sound of short a. If you have a flash card with a b and a picture of a bird on it, the picture- not the letter- becomes a signal to the child to say the b sound. The child goes through an extra step in associating the sound with the letter. Instead of looking at a b and forming the b sound, the mental process becomes "B... bird... b." This is slow, and in many cases the child stays slow because she becomes dependent on the clue. Without the clue, she has no idea how to "break" the code of the word. There's an easier way.*"

And lastly I do not use color on the pages because I believe the patterns and shapes of the letters just simply stand out better; less distraction, and I believe allowing them to color it in is extremely healthy for their hand-eye coordination, the wiring of the brain, using and exploring their senses, making decisions on what colors they want, learning what they like, and making a piece of art can be very stimulating and relaxing. In a sense, like they say music is to the brain.

In this workbook they are able to observe and study the letters and the pattern the letters make, first. We are always showing the letter, saying the letter, and writing it. In a sense they are learning the letter code.

If you have any questions or need help go to www.SpongyLittleMinds.com!

LET'S PLUNGE INTO THE BASICS

www.SpongyLittleMinds.com

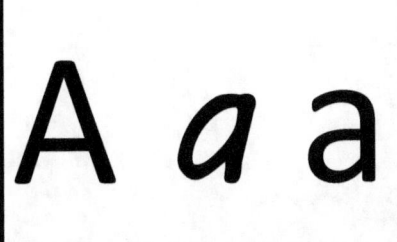

Name _____

Use a pencil or crayon to trace the big "A's" and little "a's" inside the lines.

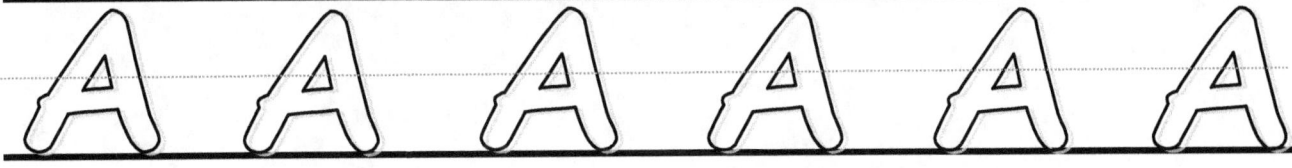

Color and cut out the big "A" and little "a" at the bottom page, then match and paste in the box.

www.SpongyLittleMinds.com

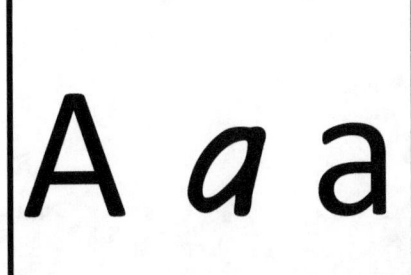

Name _____

Trace and follow the arrows. Then write your own big "A's" and little "a's" the same way.

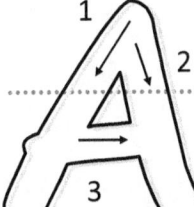

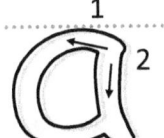

Find and put an X on big "A" and little "a".

B a b c a d a a

A B A b D B A C

www.SpongyLittleMinds.com

_____
Name

Trace and follow the arrows. Then write your own big "A's" and little "a's" the same way.

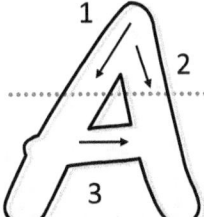

See if you can find and circle the big "A's" and little "a's" in these words. Parent note: Do not worry about the sounds of the words or what they say, this is more like a game for your child.

angels	art	alphabet	creation
Abraham	animal	atom	space
ant	Adam	antelope	apple
Isaac	Abel	apricot	Ambulance
asteroid	abacus	Cain	acrobat

www.SpongyLittleMinds.com

Name _____

Trace and follow the arrows. Then write your own big "A's" and little "a's" the same way.

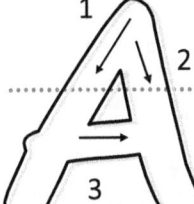

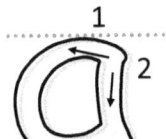

Using a pencil or crayon, find big "A" and little "a" (there are two), draw a line to connect them.

D   *a*

A   a

B   c

www.SpongyLittleMinds.com

B b

_____ Name

Use a pencil or crayon to trace the big "B's" and little "b's" inside the lines.

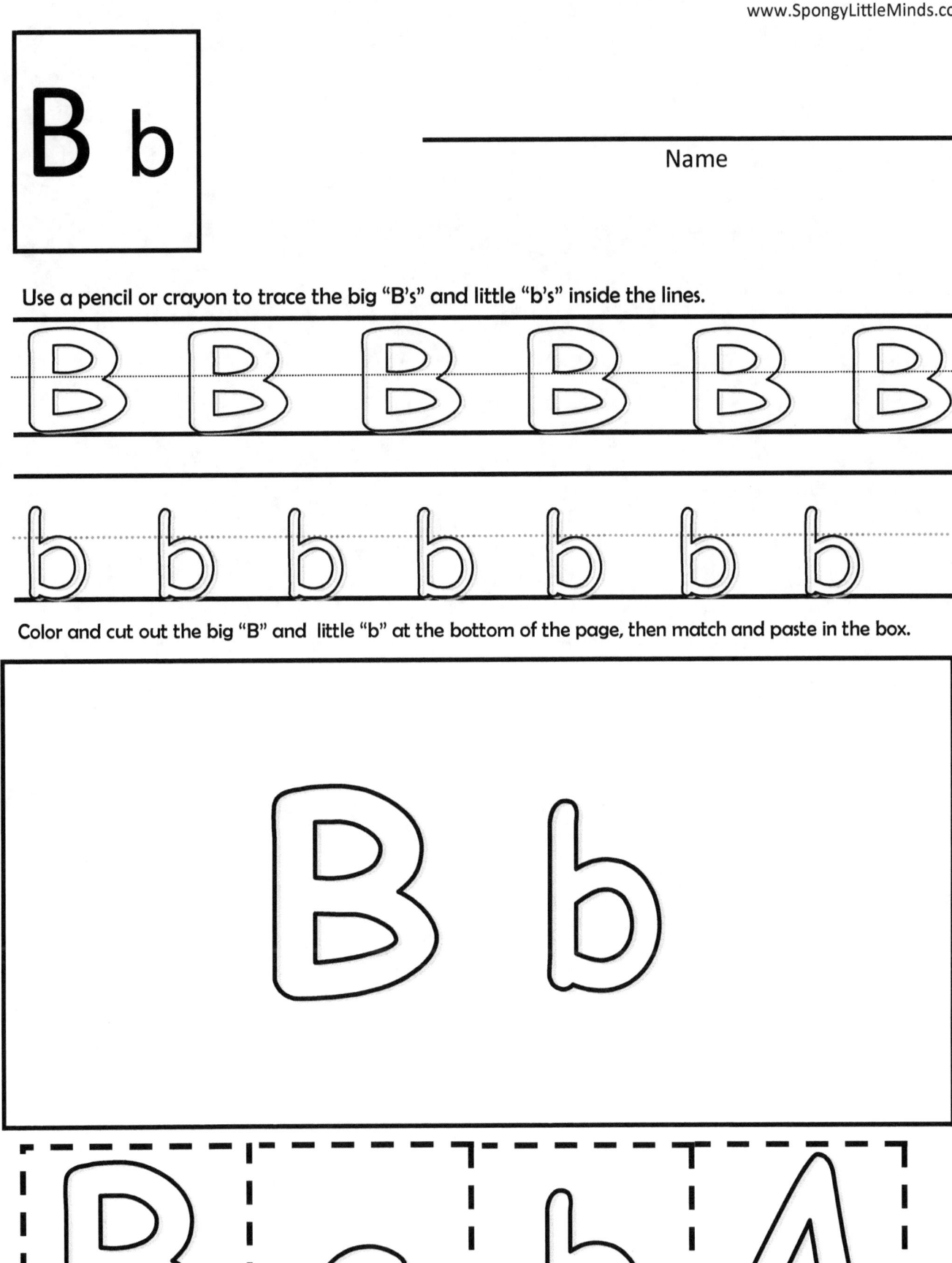

Color and cut out the big "B" and little "b" at the bottom of the page, then match and paste in the box.

www.SpongyLittleMinds.com

B b

Name _____

Trace and follow the arrows. Then write your own big "B's" and little "b's" the same way.

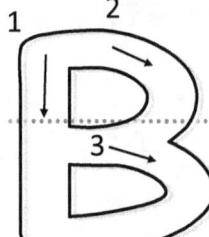

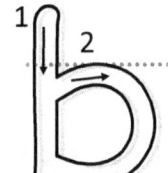

Find and put an X on big "B" and little "b".

b a b c a b a D

A B A B D B A C

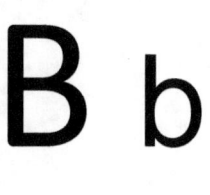

www.SpongyLittleMinds.com

_____
Name

Trace and follow the arrows. Then write your own big "B's" and little "b's" the same way.

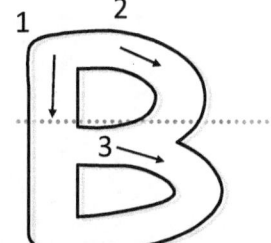

See if you can find and circle the big "B's" and little "b's" in these words. Parent note: Do not worry about the sounds of the words or what they say, this is more like a game for your child.

Bible	art	bear	creation
Abraham	Benjamin	atom	berry
baby	Adam	bullfrog	Brenda
bee	bubble	Cain	bread
balloon	brown	Bobbi	butterfly

www.SpongyLittleMinds.com

B b

_____
Name

Trace and follow the arrows. Then write your own big "B's" and little "b's" the same way.

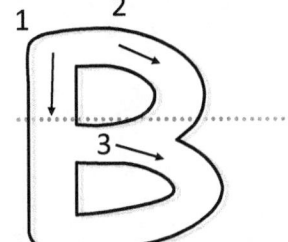

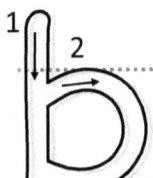

Using a crayon, find big "B" and little "b", draw a line to connect them. If you want, you could use a different color to connect big "A" and little "a" too.

B   a
C   e
A   b

www.SpongyLittleMinds.com

C c

_____ Name

Use a pencil or crayon to trace the big "C's" and little "c's" inside the lines.

C C C C C C

c c c c c c c

Color and cut out the big "C" and little "c" at the bottom of the page, then match and paste in the box.

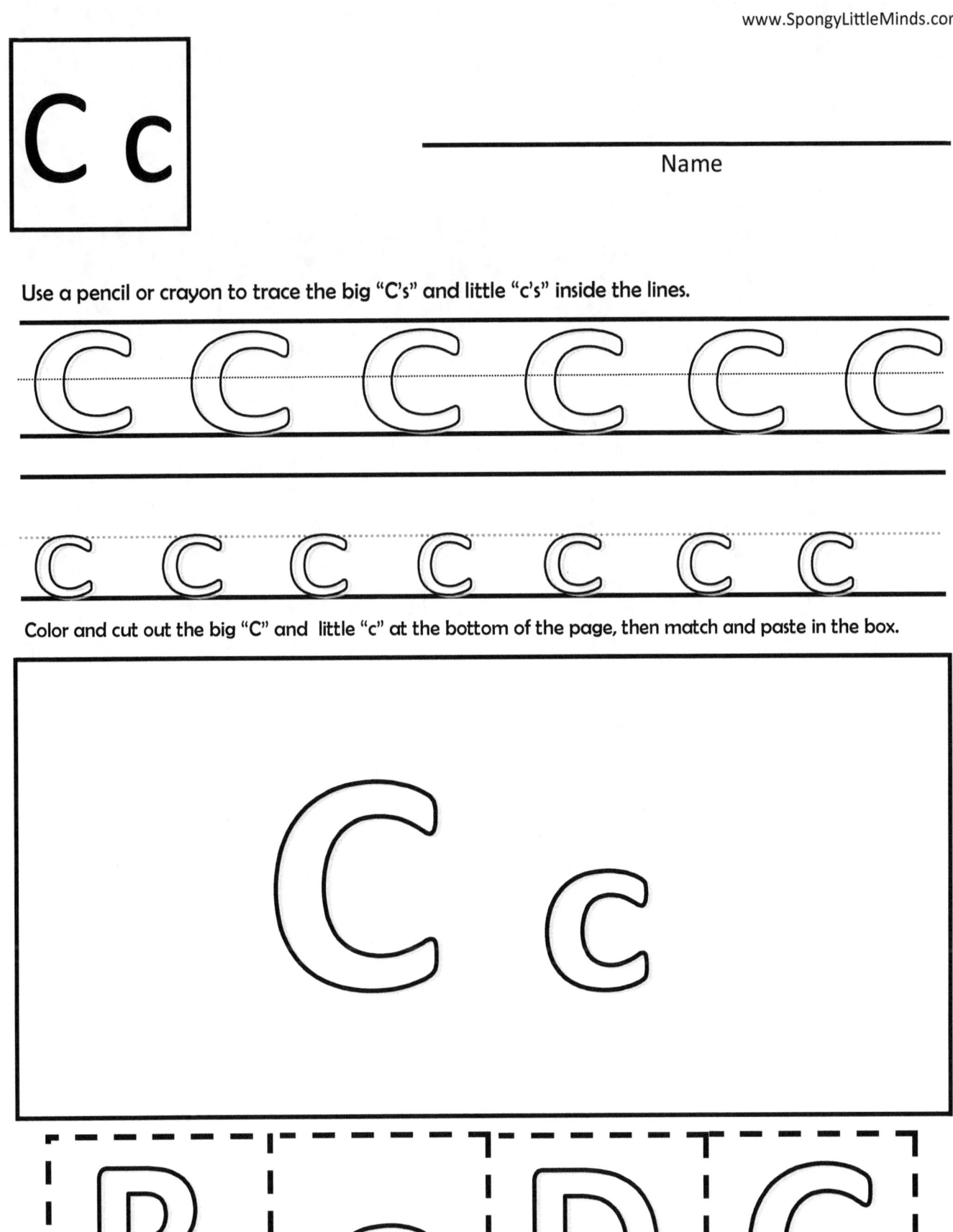

www.SpongyLittleMinds.com

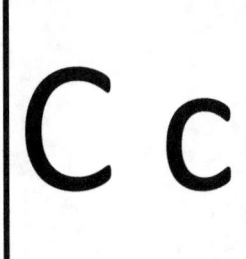

_____
Name

Trace and follow the arrows. Then write your own big "C's" and little "c's" the same way.

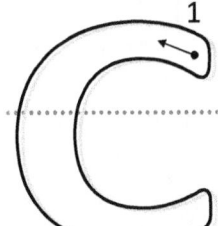

Find and put an X on big "C" and little "c".

b c b c a c c d

C B C B D C A C

www.SpongyLittleMinds.com

| C c |

_____
Name

Trace and follow the arrows. Then write your own big "C's" and little "c's" the same way.

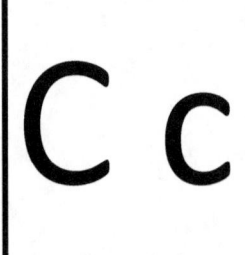

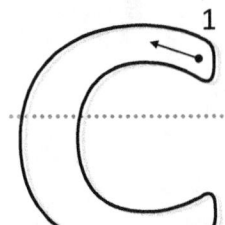

See if you can find and circle the big "C's" and little "c's" in these words. Parent note: Do not worry about the sounds of the words or what they say, this is more like a game for your child.

Bible	cricket	crayon	cabin
Creation	Benjamin	castle	berry
baby	Cross	bullfrog	cactus
camel	bubble	Cain	bread
balloon	crab	candle	Carolina

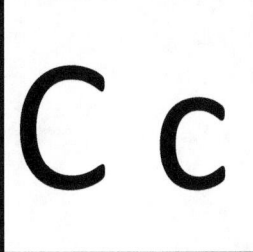

www.SpongyLittleMinds.com

_____
Name

Trace and follow the arrows. Then write your own big "C's" and little "c's" the same way.

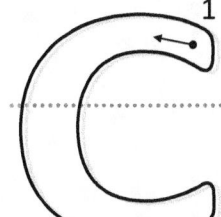

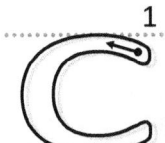

Using a crayon, find big "C" and little "c", draw a line to connect them. If you want, you could use a different color to connect big "B" and little "b" too.

B   b
C   e
A   c

www.SpongyLittleMinds.com

D d

Name _____

Use a pencil or crayon to trace the big "D's" and little "d's" inside the lines.

D D D D D D

d d d d d d

Color and cut out the big "D" and little "d" at the bottom of the page, then match and paste in the box.

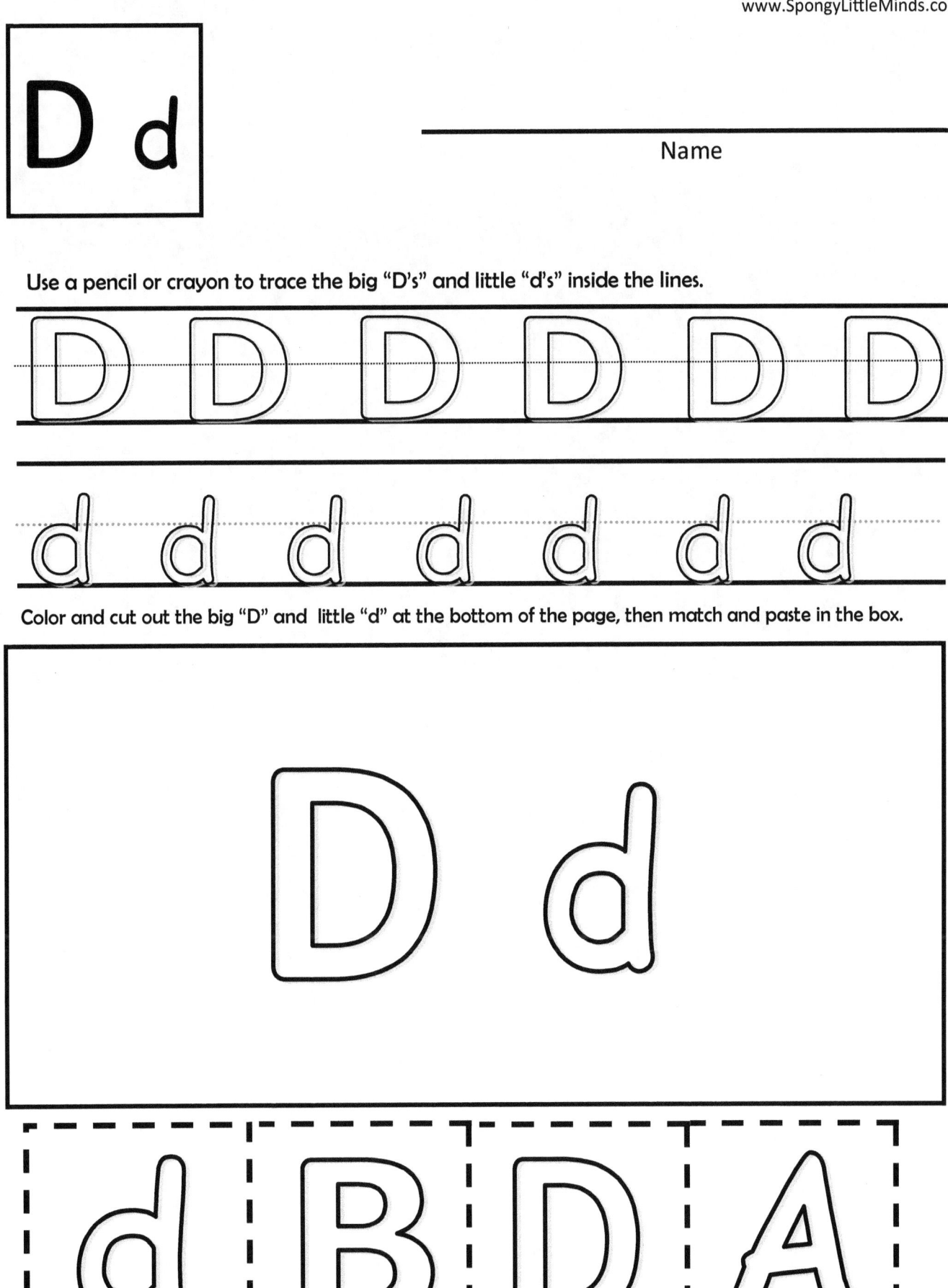

Dd

www.SpongyLittleMinds.com

_____ Name

Trace and follow the arrows. Then write your own big "D's" and little "d's" the same way.

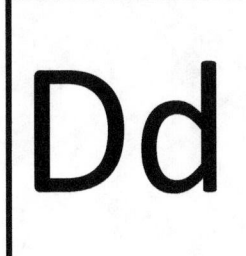

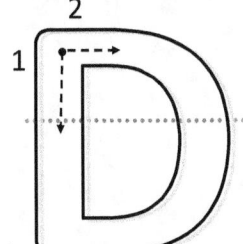

Find and put an X on little "d" and big "D".

d h d c d c e d

c D C B D C D C

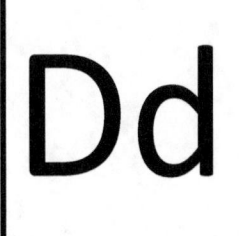

www.SpongyLittleMinds.com

_____
Name

Trace and follow the arrows. Then write your own big "D's" and little "d's" the same way.

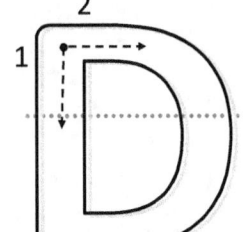

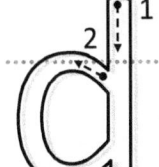

See if you can find and circle the big "D's" and little "d's" in these words. Parent note: Do not worry about the sounds of the words or what they say, this is more like a game for your child.

David	dragon	crayon	cabin
Creation	Benjamin	dandelion	Daniel
dungeon	Cross	devote	cactus
camel	Deborah	disciple	den
dinosaur	dove	candle	dedicate

www.SpongyLittleMinds.com

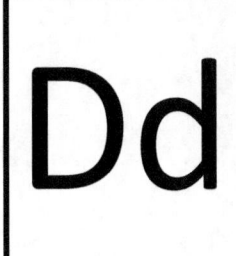

_____ Name

Trace and follow the arrows. Then write your own big "D's" and little "d's" the same way.

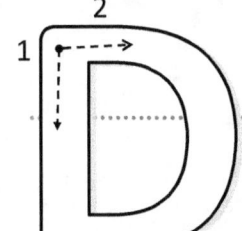

Using a crayon, find big "D" and little "d", draw a line to connect them. If you want, you could use a different color to connect big "C" and little "c" too.

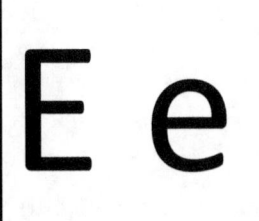

www.SpongyLittleMinds.com

_____ Name

Use a pencil or crayon to trace the big "E's" and little "e's" inside the lines.

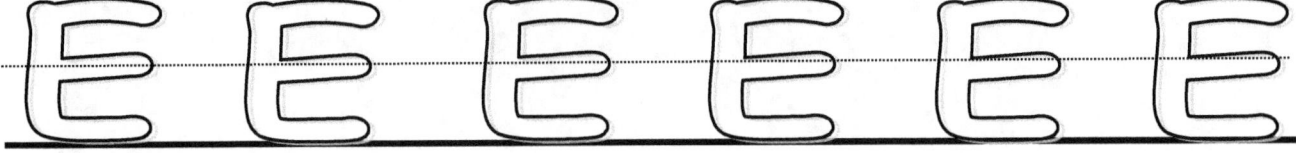

Color and cut out the big "E" and little "e" at the bottom of the page, then match and paste in the box.

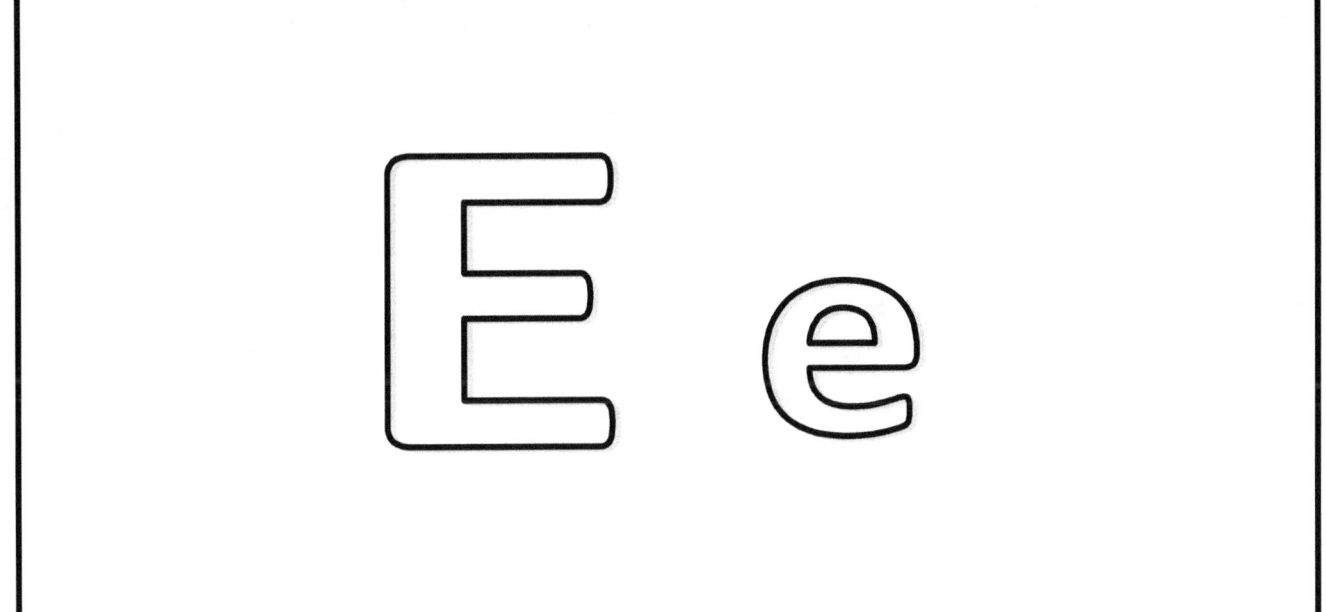

www.SpongyLittleMinds.com

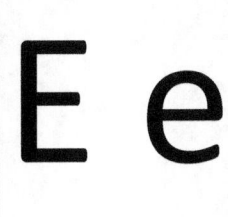

_____
Name

Trace and follow the arrows. Then write your own big "E's" and little "e's" the same way.

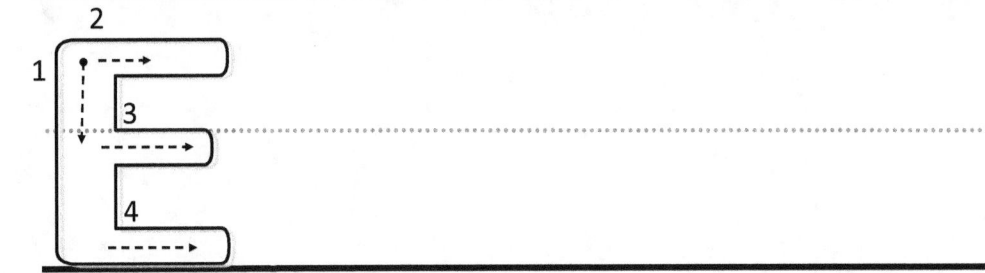

Find and put an X on little "e" and big "E".

e h d e d e e a

A D E B D E D E

www.SpongyLittleMinds.com

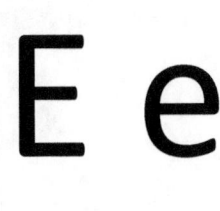

_____
Name

Trace and follow the arrows. Then write your own big "E's" and little "e's" the same way.

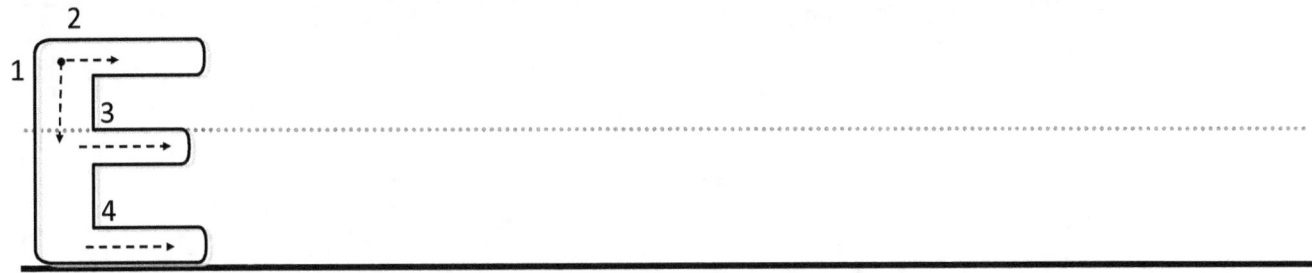

See if you can find and circle the big "E's" and little "e's" in these words. Parent note: Do not worry about the sounds of the words or what they say, this is more like a game for your child.

David	eel	Esther	cabin
Elijah	Benjamin	elephant	Daniel
dungeon	Ezekiel	devote	Enoch
eagle	Deborah	disciple	Elly
dinosaur	evening	eat	dedicate

www.SpongyLittleMinds.com

E e

_____
Name

Trace and follow the arrows. Then write your own big "E's" and little "e's" the same way.

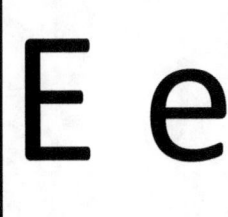

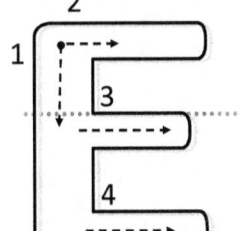

Using a crayon, find big "E" and little "e", draw a line to connect them. Use a different color to connect big "C" and little "c", and big "D" and little "d" too.

E   c

C   e

D   d

www.SpongyLittleMinds.com

_____ Name

Use a pencil or crayon to trace the big "F's" and little "f's" inside the lines.

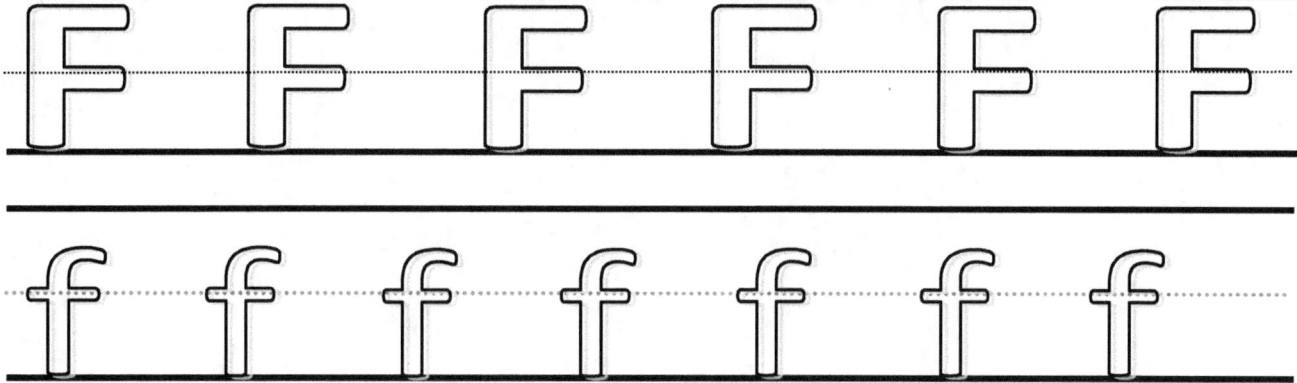

Color and cut out the big "F" and little "f" at the bottom of the page, then match and paste in the box.

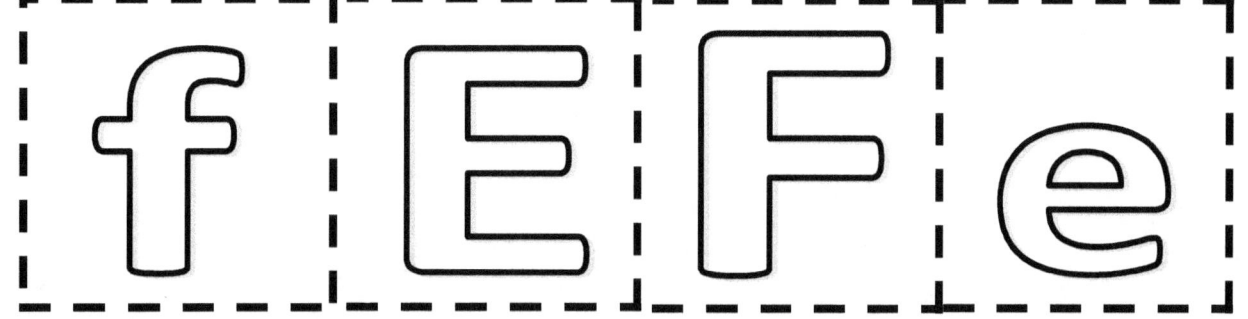

www.SpongyLittleMinds.com

_____
Name

Trace and follow the arrows. Then write your own big "F's" and little "f's" the same way.

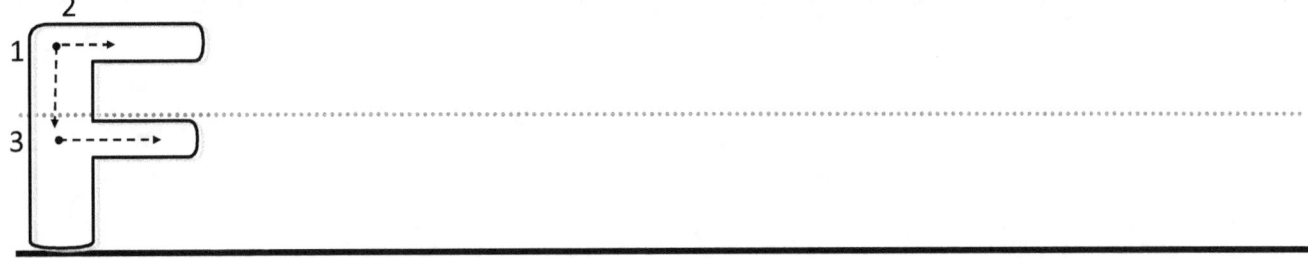

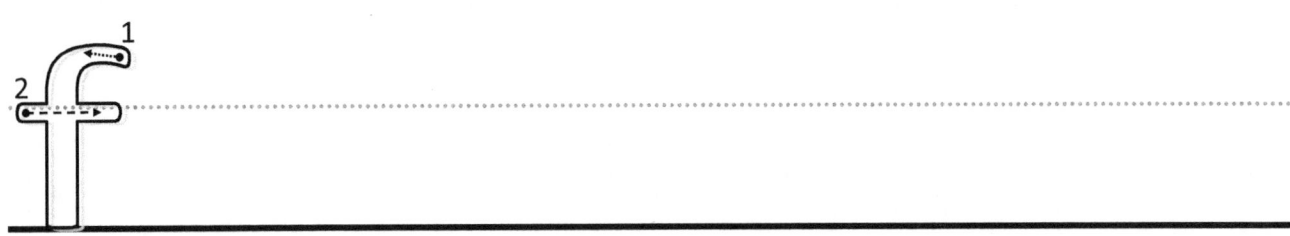

Find and put an X on little "f" and big "F".

e *f* d f *f* e f a

F̶ D F B F E D F

www.SpongyLittleMinds.com

_____
Name

Trace and follow the arrows. Then write your own big "F's" and little "f's" the same way.

See if you can find and circle the big "F's" and little "f's" in these words. Parent note: Do not worry about the sounds of the words or what they say, this is more like a game for your child.

fishermen	eel	Festus	five
Elijah	friends	elephant	Daniel
Felix	fellowship	disciple	Father
eagle	Deborah	family	fire
food	foundation	Faith	dedicate

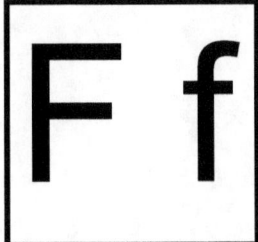

www.SpongyLittleMinds.com

_____
Name

Trace and follow the arrows. Then write your own big "F's" and little "f's" the same way.

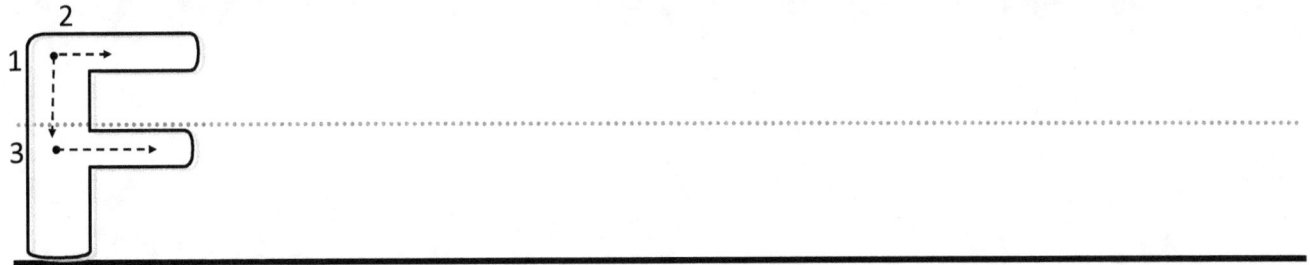

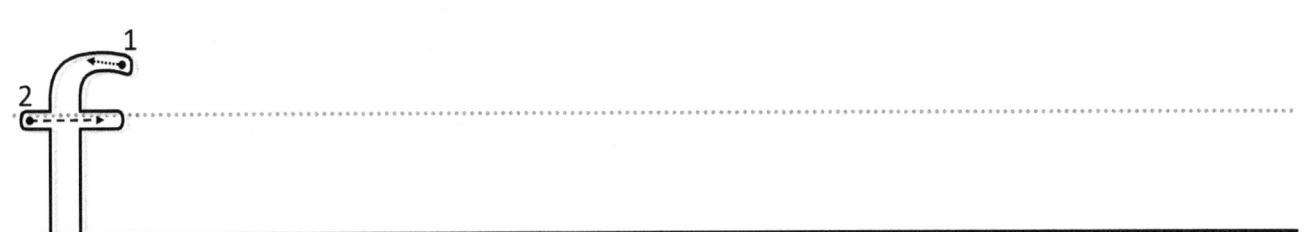

Using a crayon, find big "F" and little "f", draw a line to connect them. Use a different color to connect big "D" and little "d", and big "E" and little "e" too.

D	f
E	e
F	d

www.SpongyLittleMinds.com

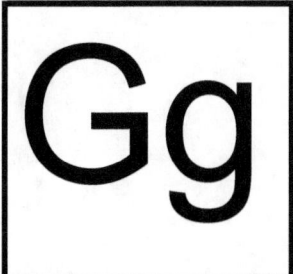

_____
Name

Use a pencil or crayon to trace the big "G's" and little "g's" inside the lines.

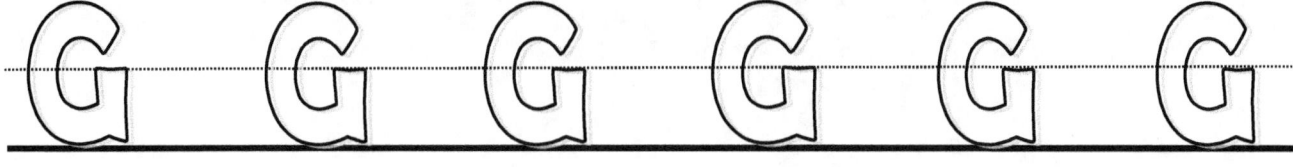

Color and cut out the big "G" and little "g" at the bottom of the page, then match and paste in the box.

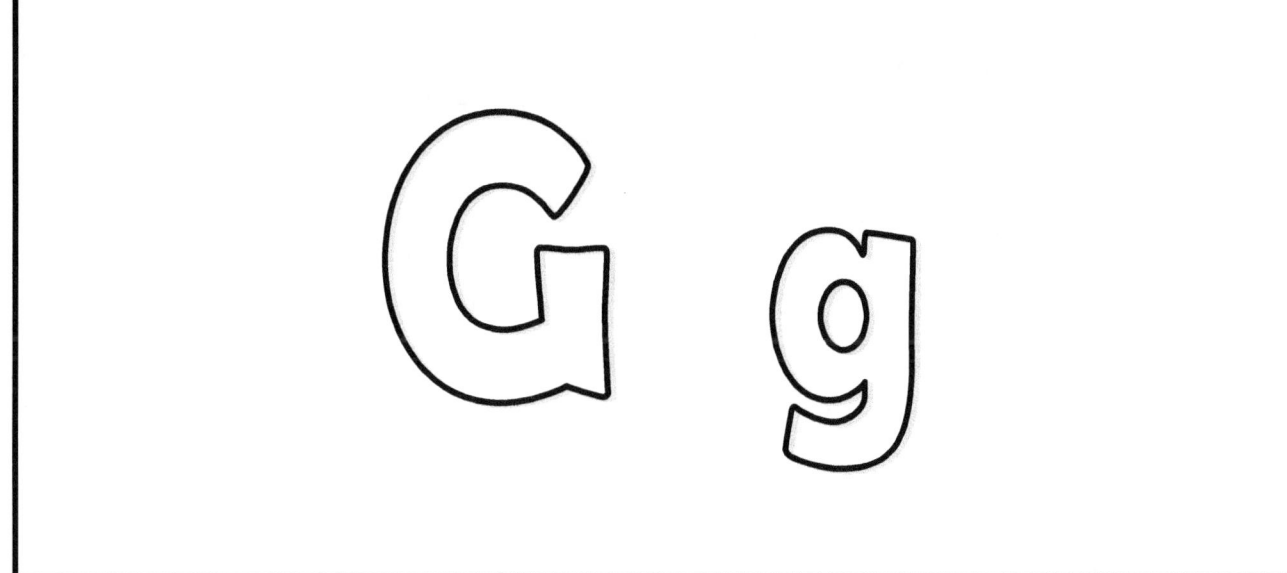

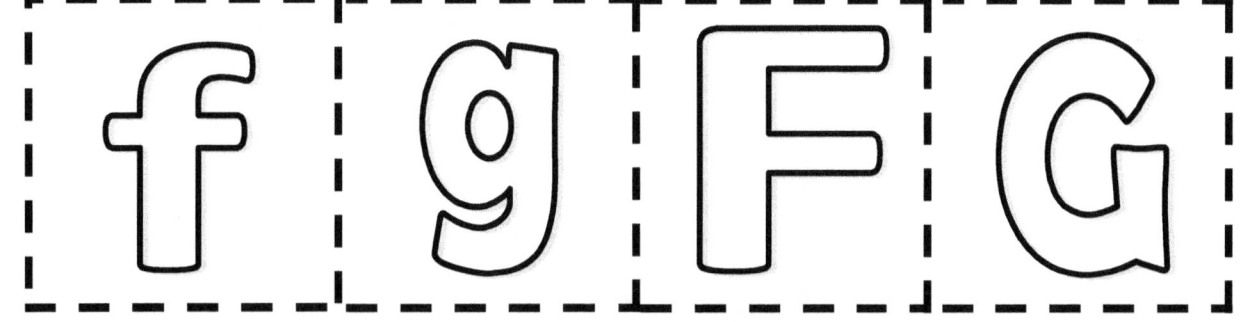

www.SpongyLittleMinds.com

_____
Name

Trace and follow the arrows. Then write your own big "G's" and little "g's" the same way.

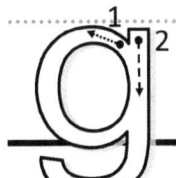

Find and put an X on little "g" and big "G".

g c g f b g f g

F G D G F G G F

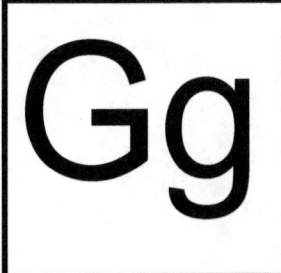

www.SpongyLittleMinds.com

_____
Name

Trace and follow the arrows. Then write your own big "G's" and little "g's" the same way.

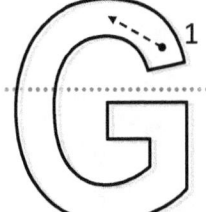

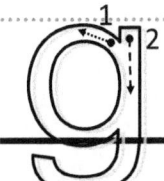

See if you can find and circle the big "G's" and little "g's" in these words. Parent note: Do not worry about the sounds of the words or what they say, this is more like a game for your child.

Gideon	goat	Festus	giraffe
fishermen	friends	Gabriel	five
gold	God	disciple	grace
eagle	Deborah	goose	fire
goodness	gift	Faith	Genesis

www.SpongyLittleMinds.com

_____
Name

Trace and follow the arrows. Then write your own big "G's" and little "g's" the same way.

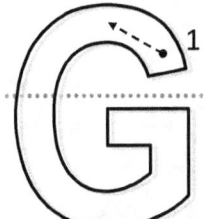

Using a crayon, find big "G" and little "g", draw a line to connect them. Use a different color to connect big "E" and little "e", and big "F" and little "f" too.

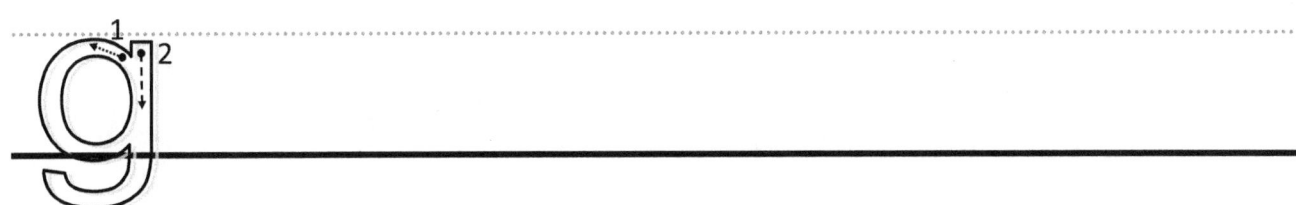

www.SpongyLittleMinds.com

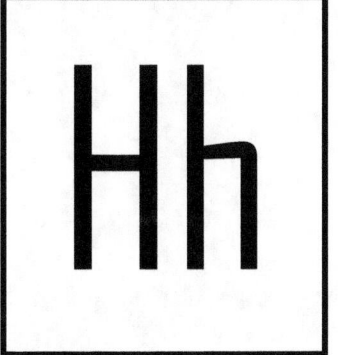

Name _____

Use a pencil or crayon to trace the big "H's" and little "h's" inside the lines.

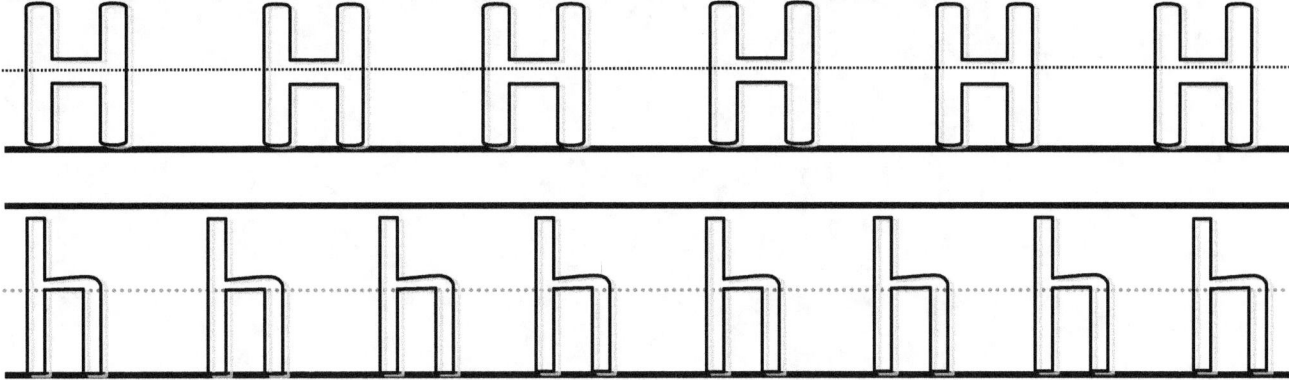

Color and cut out the big "H" and little "h" at the bottom of the page, then match and paste in the box.

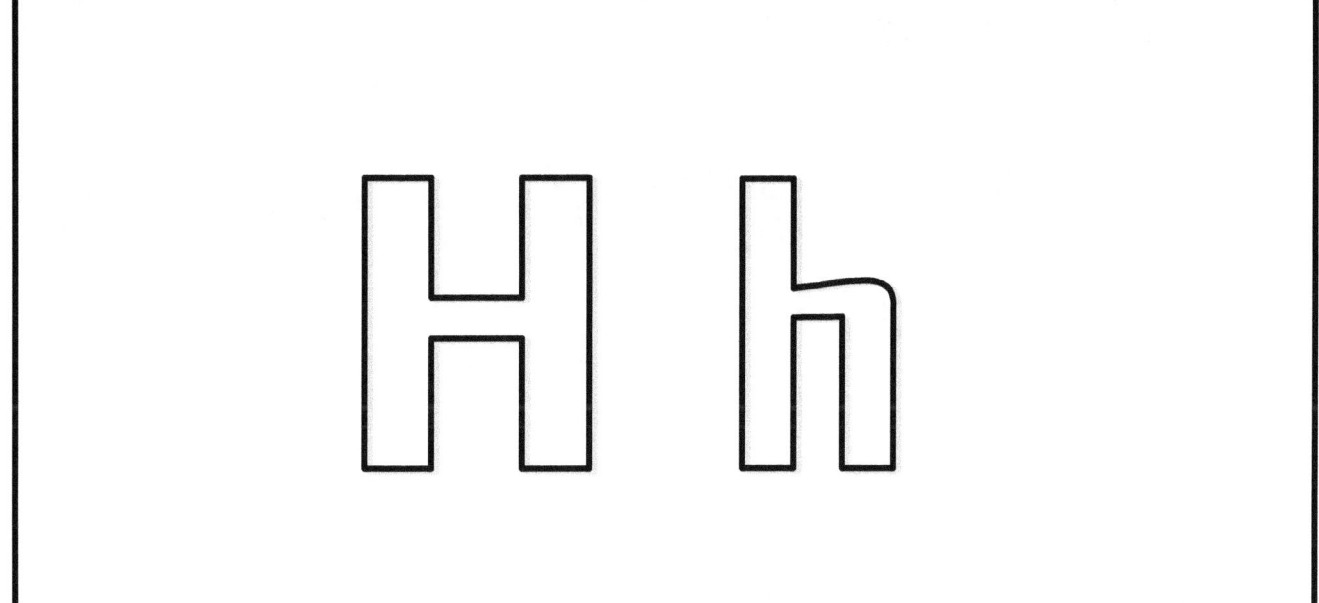

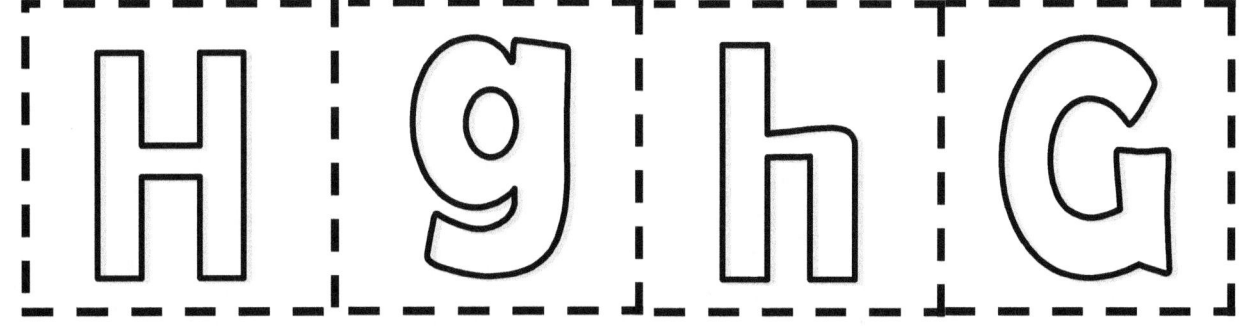

www.SpongyLittleMinds.com

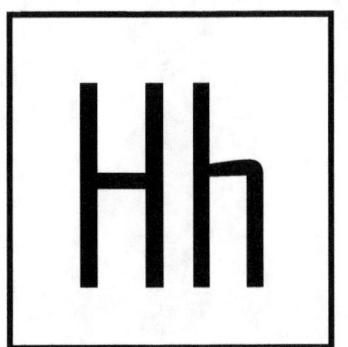

_____
Name

Trace and follow the arrows. Then write your own big "H's" and little "h's" the same way.

Find and put an X on little "h" and big "H".

g h g f *h* h f h

H G D H H G H F

www.SpongyLittleMinds.com

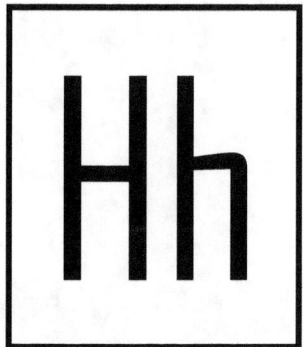

_____
Name

Trace and follow the arrows. Then write your own big "H's" and little "h's" the same way.

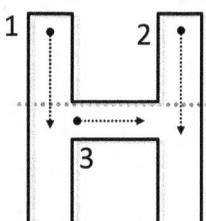

See if you can find and circle the big "H's" and little "h's" in these words. Parent note: Do not worry about the sounds of the words or what they say, this is more like a game for your child.

Gideon	goat	Habakkuk	giraffe
Holy Spirit	happy	Gabriel	hail
gold	God	hermit	grace
hallelujah	holiday	goose	herb
goodness	Hosanna	hand	Hannah

www.SpongyLittleMinds.com

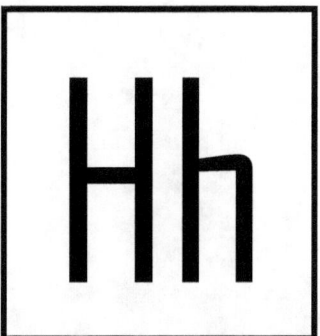

_____
Name

Trace and follow the arrows. Then write your own big "H's" and little "h's" the same way.

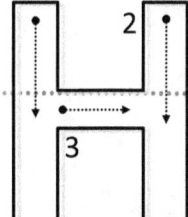

Using a crayon, find big "H" and little "h", draw a line to connect them. Use a different color to connect big "G" and little "g".

www.SpongyLittleMinds.com

Ii

_____ Name

Use a pencil or crayon to trace the big "I's" and little "i's" inside the lines.

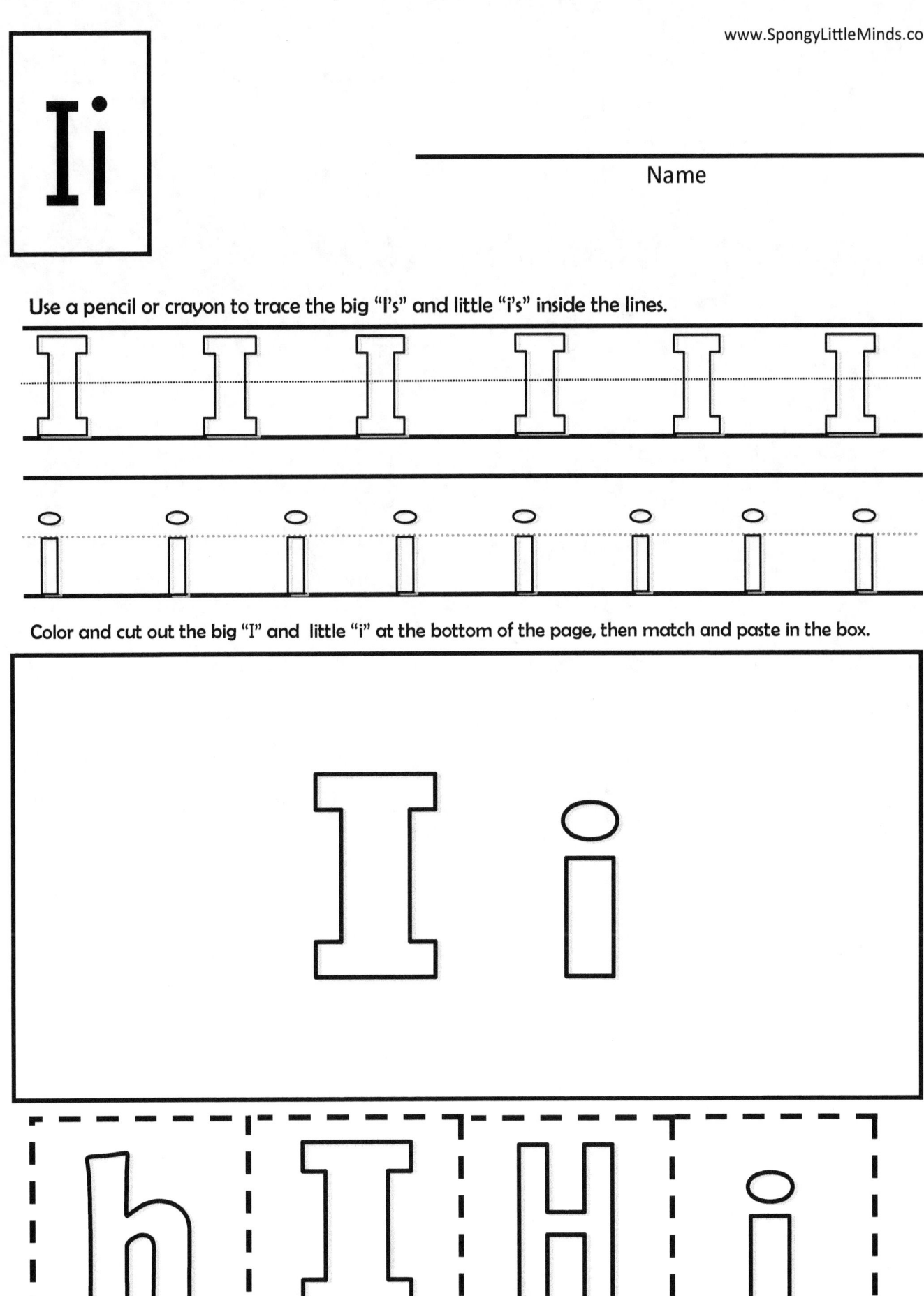

Color and cut out the big "I" and little "i" at the bottom of the page, then match and paste in the box.

www.SpongyLittleMinds.com

Name _____

Trace and follow the arrows. Then write your own big "I's" and little "i's" the same way.

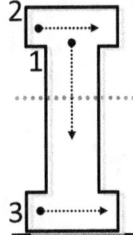

Find and put an X on little "i" and big "I".

www.SpongyLittleMinds.com

_____ Name

Trace and follow the arrows. Then write your own big "I's" and little "i's" the same way.

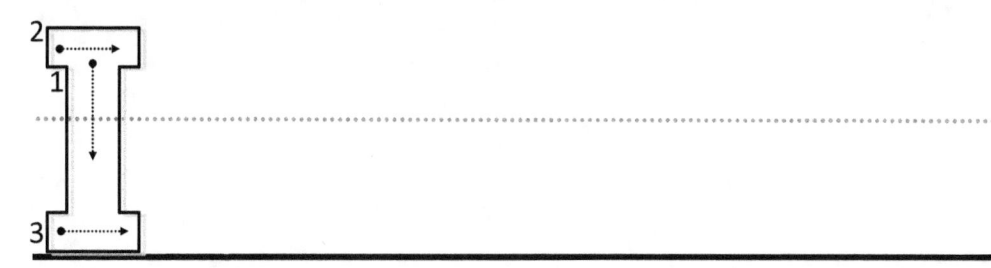

See if you can find and circle the big "I's" and little "i's" in these words. Parent note: Do not worry about the sounds of the words or what they say, this is more like a game for your child.

Isaac	goat	image	Israel
Holy Spirit	Isabelle	idol	hail
ivory	God	hermit	insect
hallelujah	inherit	Iran	herb
iron	immoral	hand	ink

www.SpongyLittleMinds.com

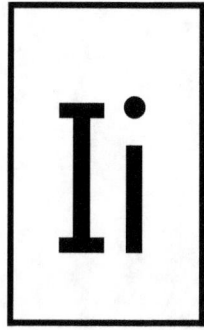

_____ Name

Trace and follow the arrows. Then write your own big "I's" and little "i's" the same way.

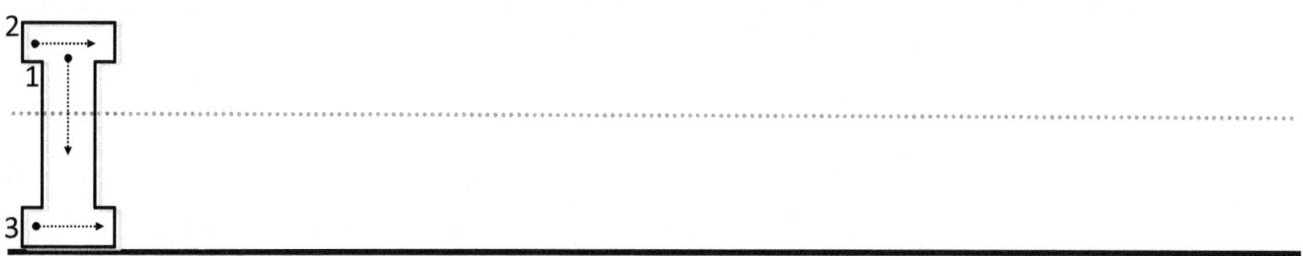

Using a crayon, find big "I" and little "i", draw a line to connect them. Use a different color to connect big "H" and little "h", and still another color to connect big "G" and little "g".

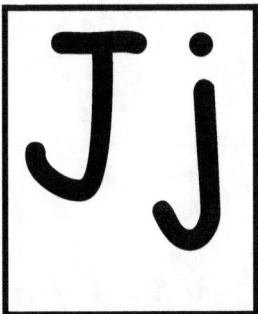

www.SpongyLittleMinds.com

_____ Name

Use a pencil or crayon to trace the big "J's" and little "j's" inside the lines.

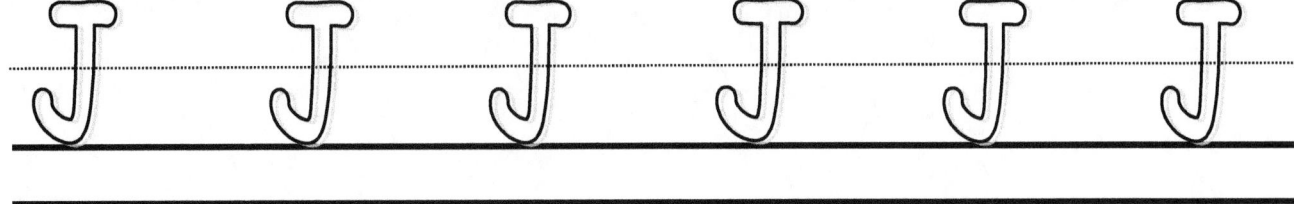

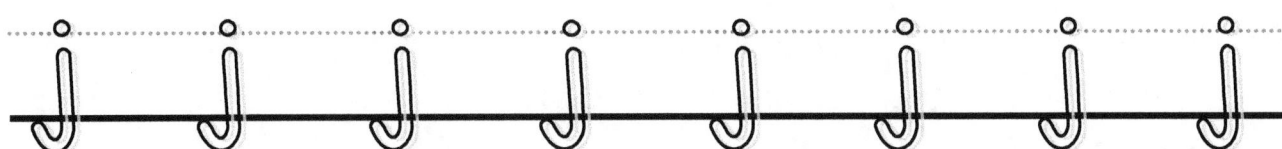

Color and cut out the big "J" and little "j" at the bottom of the page, then match and paste in the box.

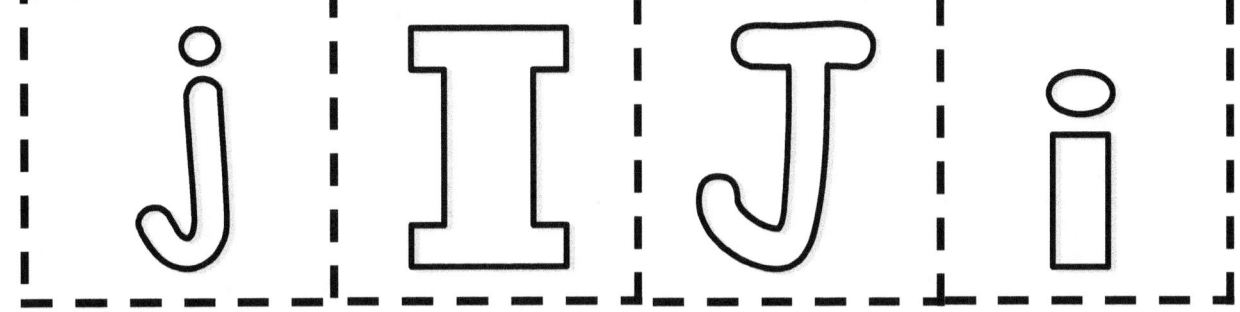

www.SpongyLittleMinds.com

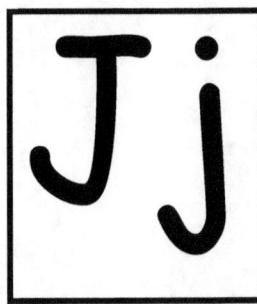

_____
Name

Trace and follow the arrows. Then write your own big "J's" and little "j's" the same way.

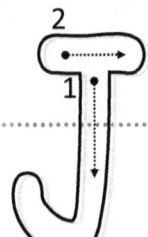

Find and put an X on little "j" and big "J".

i j i j h i j i

J I J I J J H I

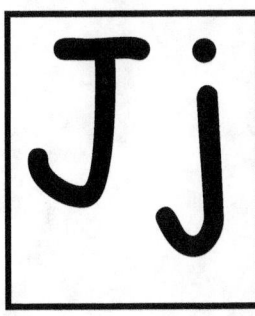

www.SpongyLittleMinds.com

_____
Name

Trace and follow the arrows. Then write your own big "J's" and little "j's" the same way.

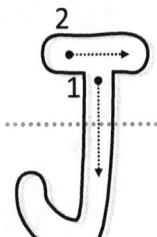

See if you can find and circle the big "J's" and little "j's" in these words. Parent note: Do not worry about the sounds of the words or what they say, this is more like a game for your child.

Isaac	job	Joseph	Israel
Jesus	Isabelle	idol	Jew
ivory	jaguar	jackrabbit	insect
jail	inherit	Iran	John
iron	Jerusalem	joy	jealous

www.SpongyLittleMinds.com

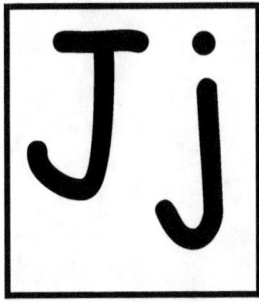

_____ Name

Trace and follow the arrows. Then write your own big "J's" and little "j's" the same way.

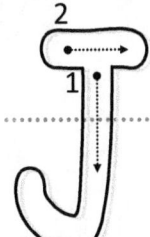

Using a crayon, find big "J" and little "j", draw a line to connect them. Use a different color to connect big "I" and little "i", and still another color to connect big "H" and little "h".

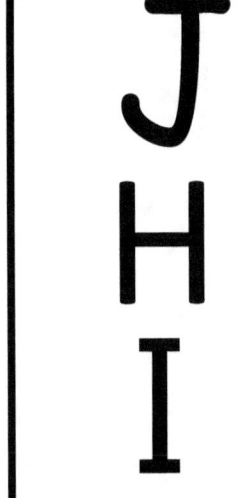

www.SpongyLittleMinds.com

_____
Name

Use a pencil or crayon to trace the big "K's" and little "k's" inside the lines.

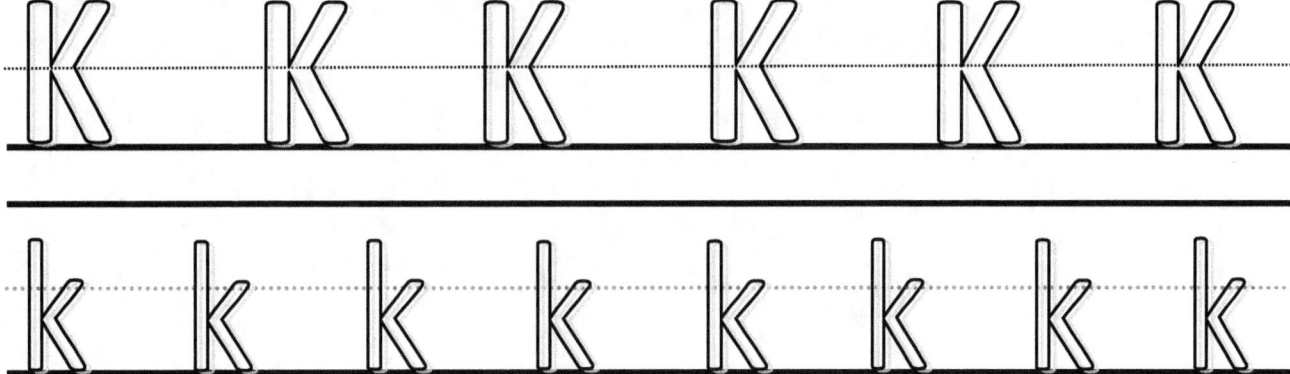

Color and cut out the big "K" and little "k" at the bottom of the page, then match and paste in the box.

www.SpongyLittleMinds.com

_____
Name

Trace and follow the arrows. Then write your own big "K's" and little "k's" the same way.

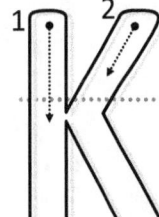

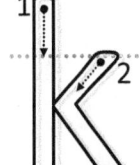

Find and put an X on little "k" and big "K".

k j k j k i j k
J K J K J K K I

www.SpongyLittleMinds.com

_____
Name

Trace and follow the arrows. Then write your own big "K's" and little "k's" the same way.

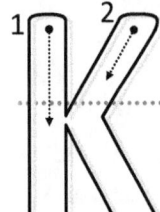

See if you can find and circle the big "K's" and little "k's" in these words. Parent note: Do not worry about the sounds of the words or what they say, this is more like a game for your child.

Kaleb	job	key	kindness
Jesus	knowledge	Keturah	Jew
knock	jaguar	jackrabbit	insect
jail	Katie	Iran	kingdom
kangaroo	Jerusalem	keeper	Kimberly

www.SpongyLittleMinds.com

_____
Name

Trace and follow the arrows. Then write your own big "K's" and little "k's" the same way.

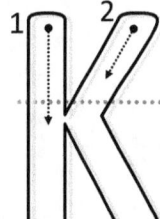

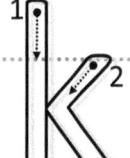

Using a crayon, find big "K" and little "k", draw a line to connect them. Use a different color to connect big "J" and little "j", and still another color to connect big "I" and little "i".

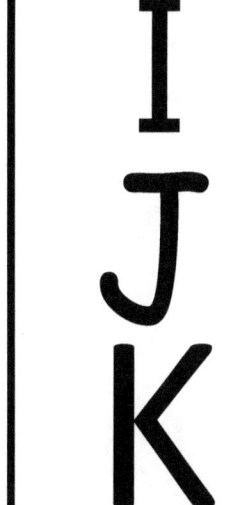

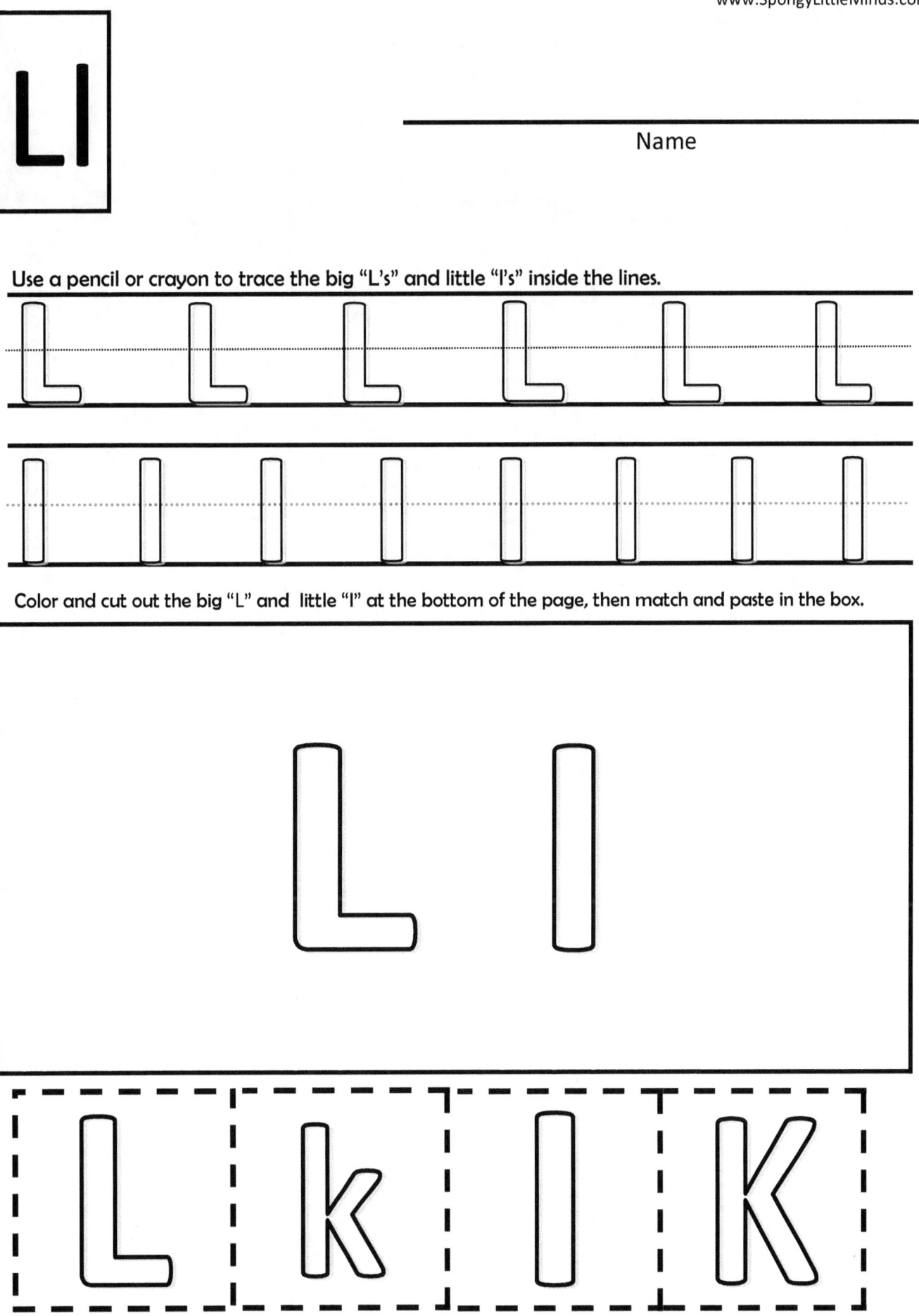

www.SpongyLittleMinds.com

Name _____

Trace and follow the arrows. Then write your own big "L's" and little "l's" the same way.

Find and put an X on little "l" and big "L".

k l k l k i l k
L K L K L K K L

www.SpongyLittleMinds.com

_____
Name

Trace and follow the arrows. Then write your own big "L's" and little "l's" the same way.

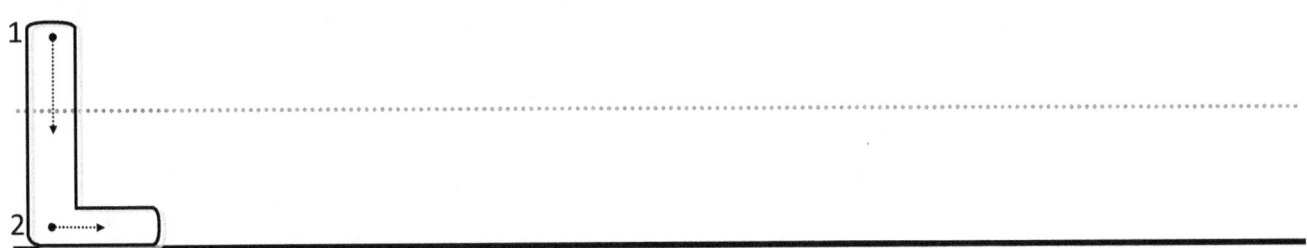

See if you can find and circle the big "L's" and little "l's" in these words. Parent note: Do not worry about the sounds of the words or what they say, this is more like a game for your child.

Luke	Lord	key	lyre
love	knowledge	cattle	Lot
knock	laugh	light	locusts
Lebanon	Katie	law	kingdom
Isaiah	life	Lazarus	lion

www.SpongyLittleMinds.com

_____ Name

Trace and follow the arrows. Then write your own big "L's" and little "l's" the same way.

Using a crayon, find big "L" and little "l", draw a line to connect them. Use a different color to connect big "K" and little "k", and still another color to connect big "J" and little "j".

www.SpongyLittleMinds.com

Name _____

Use a pencil or crayon to trace the big "M's" and little "m's" inside the lines.

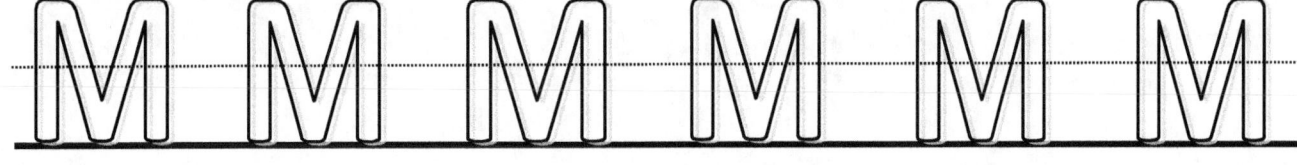

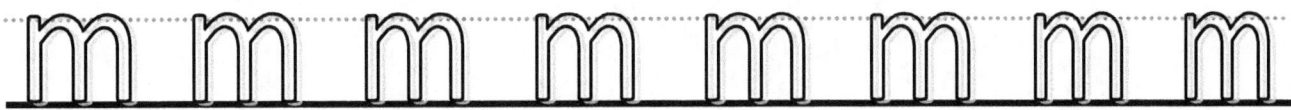

Color and cut out the big "M" and little "m" at the bottom of the page, then match and paste in the box.

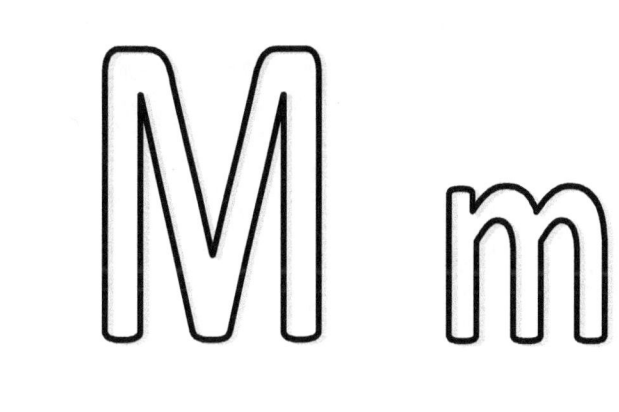

www.SpongyLittleMinds.com

Name _____

Trace and follow the arrows. Then write your own big "M's" and little "m's" the same way.

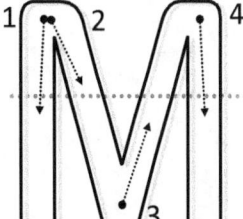

Find and put an X on little "m" and big "M".

m l m l m i l m

L M L M L M M L

www.SpongyLittleMinds.com

Name _____

Trace and follow the arrows. Then write your own big "M's" and little "m's" the same way.

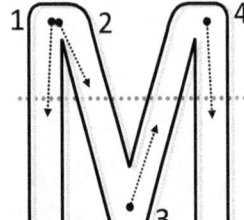

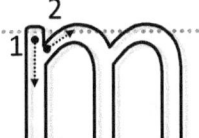

See if you can find and circle the big "M's" and little "m's" in these words. Parent note: Do not worry about the sounds of the words or what they say, this is more like a game for your child.

Luke	Messiah	key	Macedonia
Mathew	minister	mercy	Lot
Mark	laugh	light	Moses
Lebanon	Mary	miracle	manna
messenger	life	meek	lion

www.SpongyLittleMinds.com

_____
Name

Trace and follow the arrows. Then write your own big "M's" and little "m's" the same way.

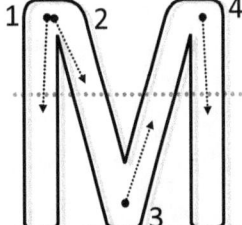

Using a crayon, find big "M" and little "m", draw a line to connect them. Use a different color to connect big "L" and little "l", and still another color to connect big "K" and little "k".

www.SpongyLittleMinds.com

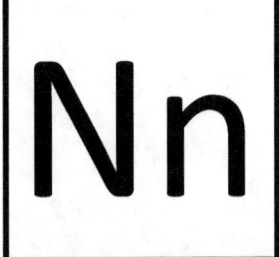

_____
Name

Use a pencil or crayon to trace the big "N's" and little "n's" inside the lines.

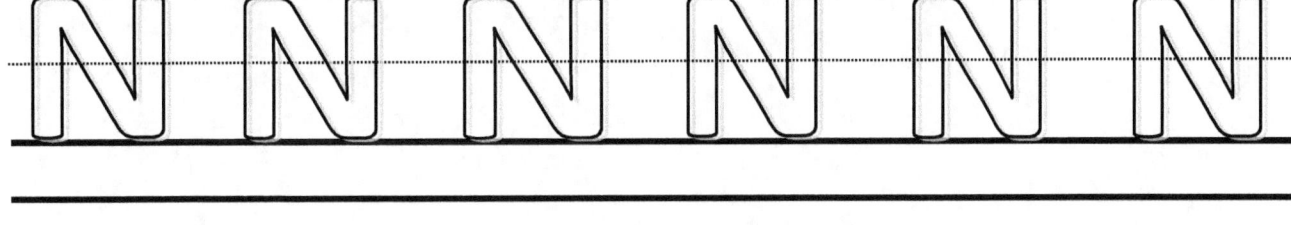

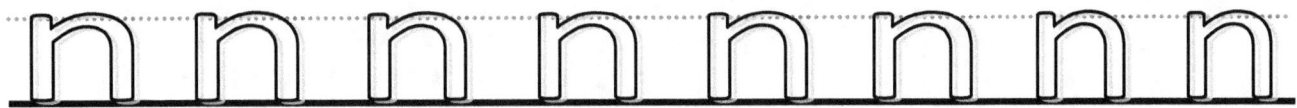

Color and cut out the big "N" and little "n" at the bottom of the page, then match and paste in the box.

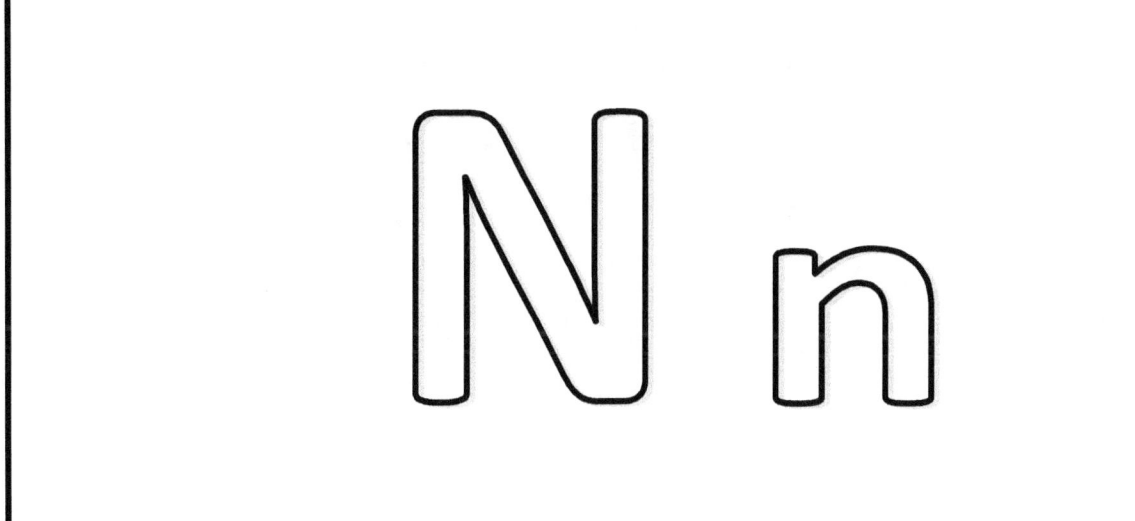

www.SpongyLittleMinds.com

Nn

_____
Name

Trace and follow the arrows. Then write your own big "N's" and little "n's" the same way.

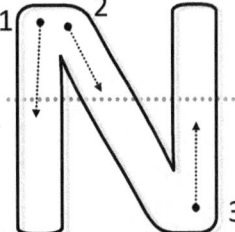

Find and put an X on little "n" and big "N".

m n m n m n n m

N M N M N M M N

www.SpongyLittleMinds.com

Name _____

Trace and follow the arrows. Then write your own big "N's" and little "n's" the same way.

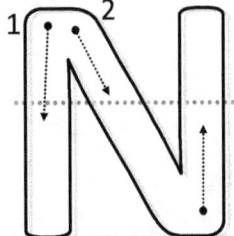

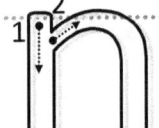

See if you can find and circle the big "N's" and little "n's" in these words. Parent note: Do not worry about the sounds of the words or what they say, this is more like a game for your child.

neighbor	Messiah	nail	Naomi
Nicodemus	Nile	mercy	numbers
Mark	noon	name	Moses
Noah	Mary	north	manna
messenger	Nebuchadnezzar	Ninevah	narwhal

www.SpongyLittleMinds.com

| **N n** |

_____
Name

Trace and follow the arrows. Then write your own big "N's" and little "n's" the same way.

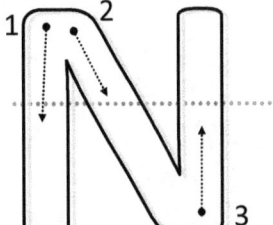

Using a crayon, find big "N" and little "n", draw a line to pair them up. Use a different color to pair up big "M" and little "m", and still another color to pair up big "L" and little "l".

| L   m |
| N |
| M   l |
| n |

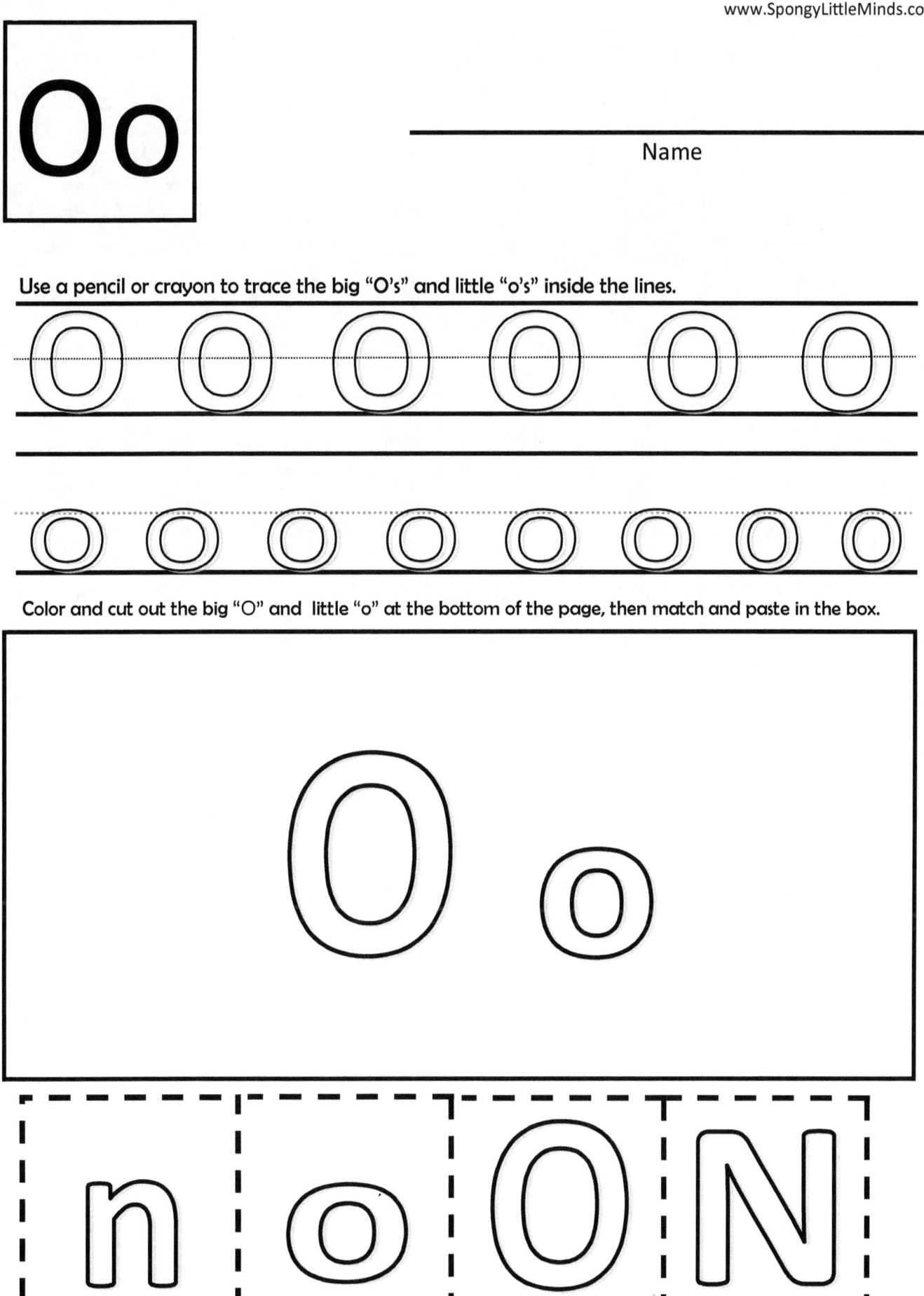

www.SpongyLittleMinds.com

_____ Name

Trace and follow the arrows. Then write your own big "O's" and little "o's" the same way.

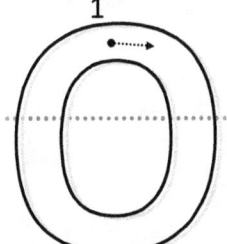

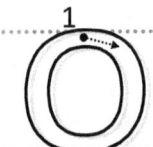

Find and put an X on little "o" and big "O".

o n m n o n o n
NONONONM

www.SpongyLittleMinds.com

_____
Name

Trace and follow the arrows. Then write your own big "O's" and little "o's" the same way.

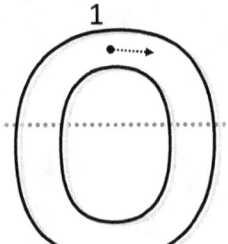

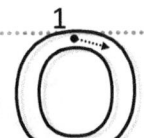

See if you can find and circle the big "O's" and little "o's" in these words. Parent note: Do not worry about the sounds of the words or what they say, this is more like a game for your child.

neighbor	Ocean	nail	Orlando
Nicodemus	Nile	otter	numbers
ostrich	open	name	Moses
Noah	obey	north	over
olive	Nebuchadnezzar	Oscar	narwhal

www.SpongyLittleMinds.com

_____
Name

Trace and follow the arrows. Then write your own big "O's" and little "o's" the same way.

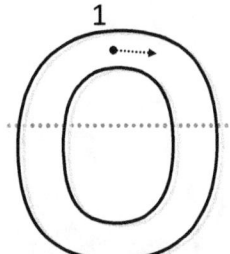

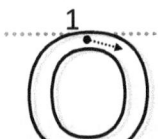

Using a crayon, find big "O" and little "o", draw a line to pair them up. Use a different color to pair up big "N" and little "n", and still another color to pair up big "M" and little "m".

www.SpongyLittleMinds.com

_____ Name

Use a pencil or crayon to trace the big "P's" and little "P's" inside the lines.

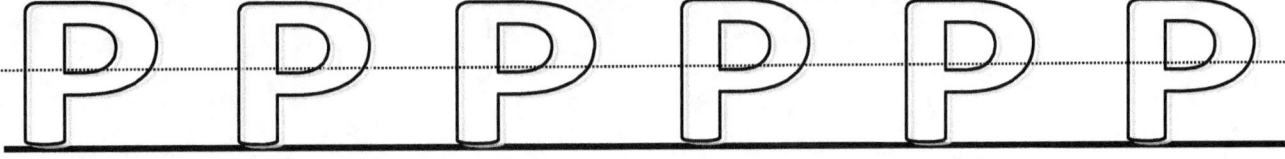

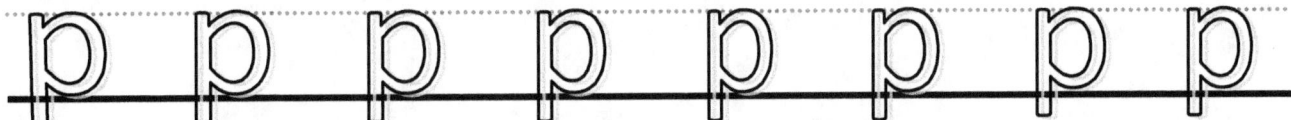

Color and cut out the big "P" and little "p" at the bottom of the page, then match and paste in the box.

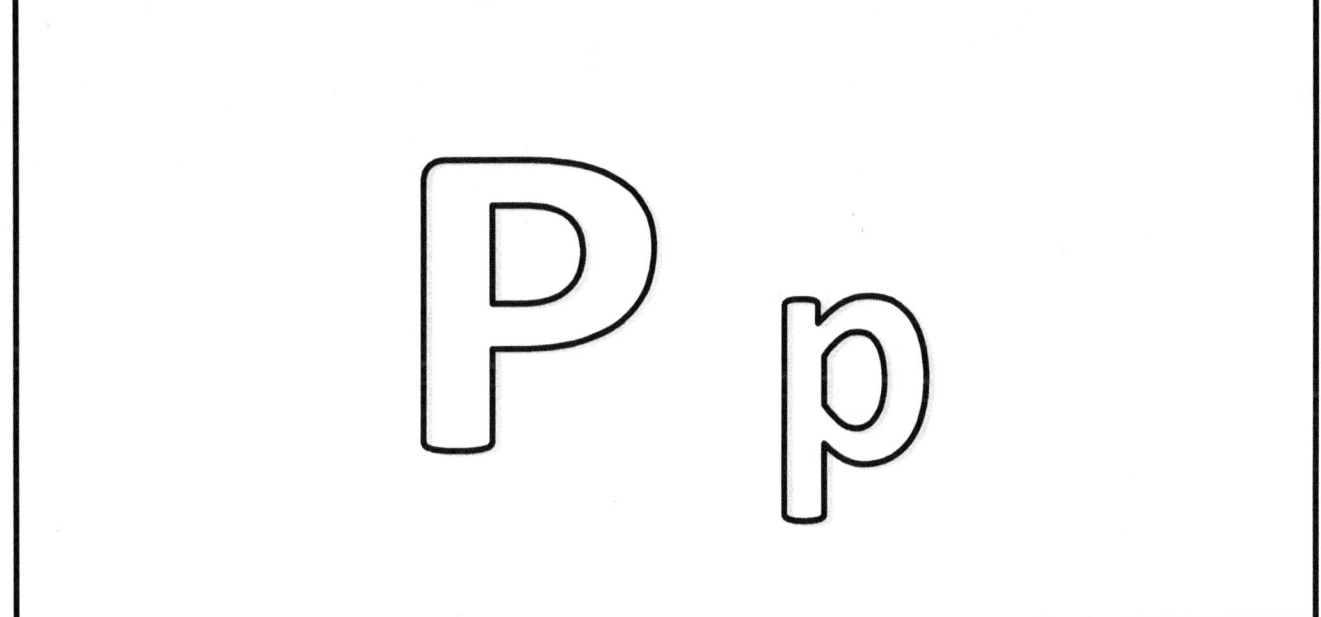

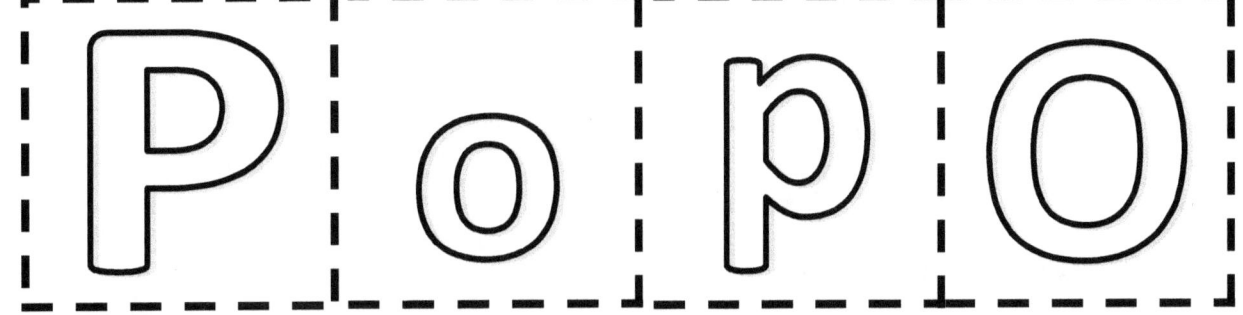

www.SpongyLittleMinds.com

_____
Name

Trace and follow the arrows. Then write your own big "P's" and little "p's" the same way.

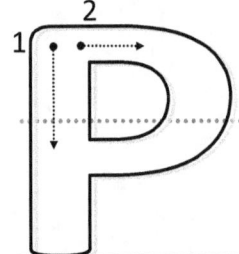

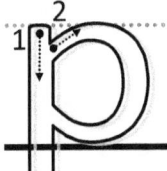

Find and put an X on little "p" and big "P".

o p m p o p o n

P O N O P O P M

www.SpongyLittleMinds.com

Pp

_____ Name

Trace and follow the arrows. Then write your own big "P's" and little "p's" the same way.

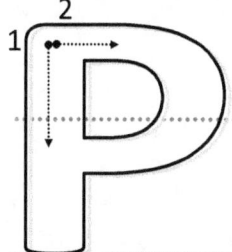

See if you can find and circle the big "P's" and little "p's" in these words. Parent note: Do not worry about the sounds of the words or what they say, this is more like a game for your child.

parents	Messiah	patience	Persia
Paul	Proverbs	mercy	popcorn
Mark	people	peace	Moses
Peter	Mary	north	manna
messenger	Passover	Philip	praise

www.SpongyLittleMinds.com

_____
Name

Trace and follow the arrows. Then write your own big "P's" and little "p's" the same way.

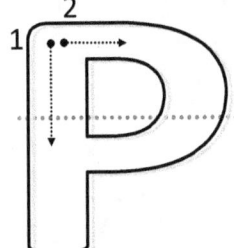

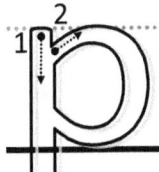

Using a crayon, find big "P" and little "p", draw a line to pair them up. Use a different color to pair up big "O" and little "o", and still another color to pair up big "N" and little "n".

www.SpongyLittleMinds.com

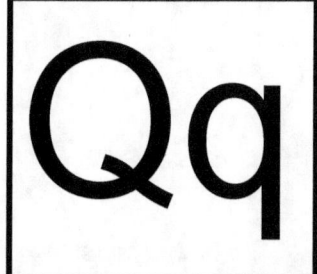

_____
Name

Use a pencil or crayon to trace the big "Q's" and little "q's" inside the lines.

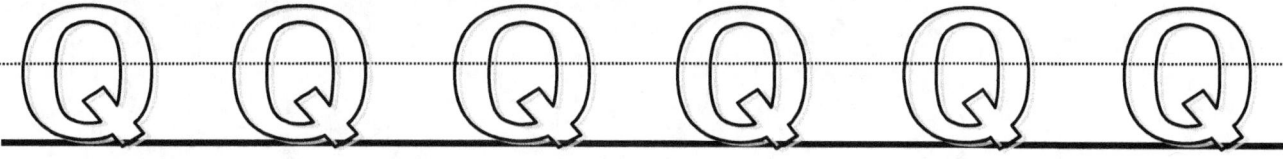

Color and cut out the big "Q" and little "q" at the bottom of the page, then match and paste in the box.

www.SpongyLittleMinds.com

_____
Name

Trace and follow the arrows. Then write your own big "Q's" and little "q's" the same way.

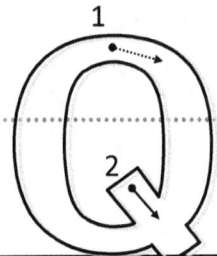

Find and put an X on little "q" and big "Q".

q p q p o p q q
P Q Q O Q O P Q

www.SpongyLittleMinds.com

_____
Name

Trace and follow the arrows. Then write your own big "Q's" and little "q's" the same way.

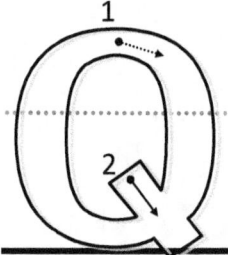

See if you can find and circle the big "Q's" and little "q's" in these words. Parent note: Do not worry about the sounds of the words or what they say, this is more like a game for your child.

Queen	quill	quest	Persia
Paul	quick	quarry	quarter
quiet	people	peace	praise
Peter	quilt	north	quail
question	Passover	Quebec	quart

www.SpongyLittleMinds.com

_____
Name

Trace and follow the arrows. Then write your own big "Q's" and little "q's" the same way.

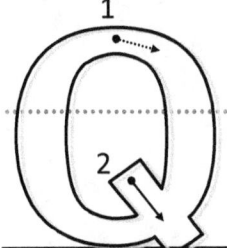

Using a crayon, find big "Q" and little "q", draw a line to pair them up. Use a different color to pair up big "P" and little "p", and still another color to pair up big "O" and little "o".

Q   p
O   q
P   o

www.SpongyLittleMinds.com

_____ Name

Use a pencil or crayon to trace the big "R's" and little "r's" inside the lines.

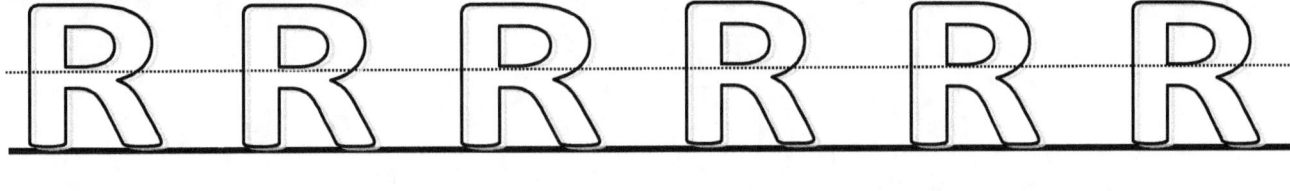

Color and cut out the big "R" and little "r" at the bottom of the page, then match and paste in the box.

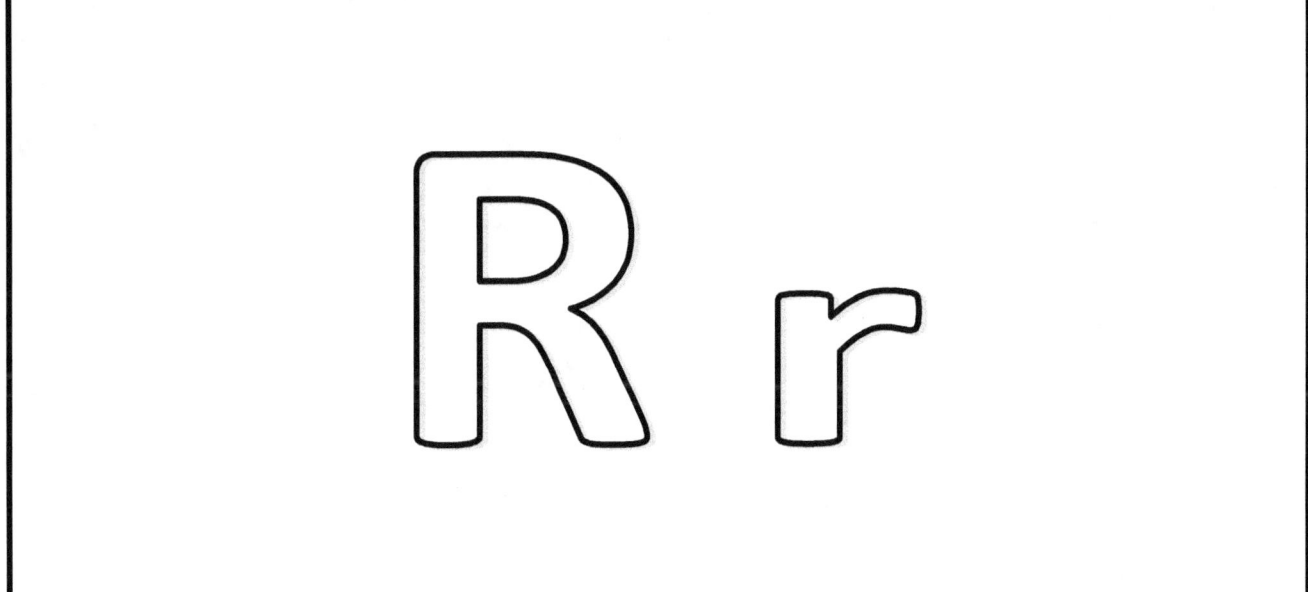

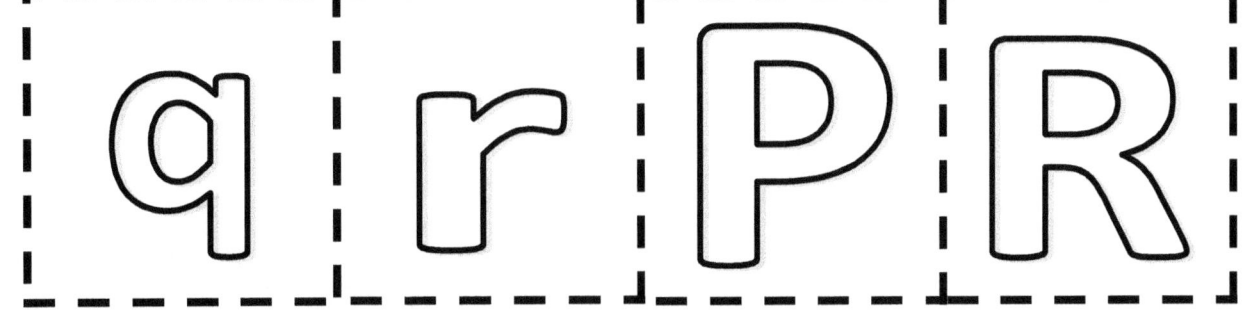

www.SpongyLittleMinds.com

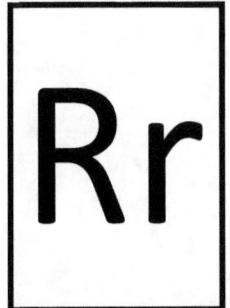

_____
Name

Trace and follow the arrows. Then write your own big "R's" and little "r's" the same way.

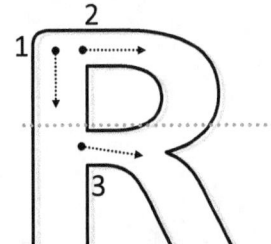

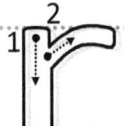

Find and put an X on little "r" and big "R".

q r q p r r q r

P R Q R Q R P R

www.SpongyLittleMinds.com

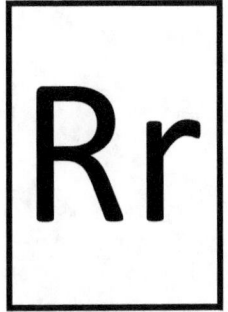

Name _____

Trace and follow the arrows. Then write your own big "R's" and little "r's" the same way.

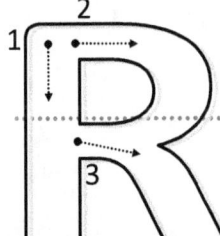

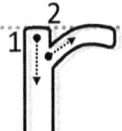

See if you can find and circle the big "R's" and little "r's" in these words. Parent note: Do not worry about the sounds of the words or what they say, this is more like a game for your child.

rainbow	rhinoceros	revive	Persia
Revelation	quick	quarry	quarter
quiet	rain	Rameses	river
Peter	quilt	rest	Rebekah
reveal	resurrection	Passover	quart

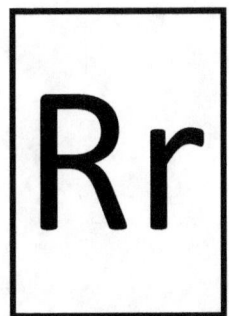

www.SpongyLittleMinds.com

_____
Name

Trace and follow the arrows. Then write your own big "R's" and little "r's" the same way.

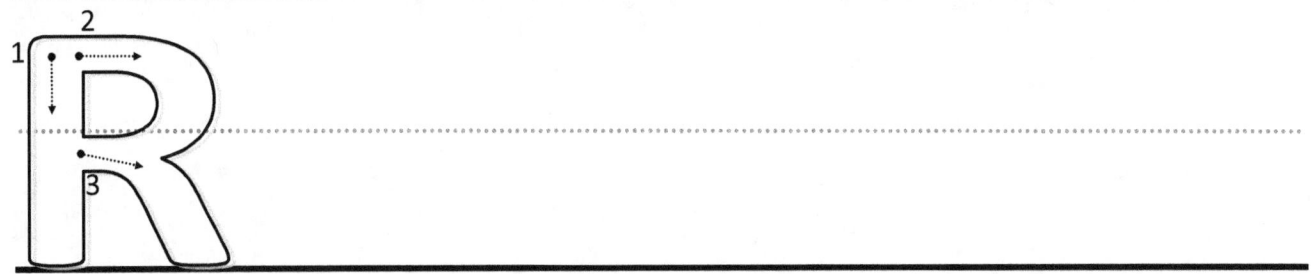

Using a crayon, find big "R" and little "r", draw a line to pair them up. Use a different color to pair up big "Q" and little "q", and still another color to pair up big "P" and little "p".

www.SpongyLittleMinds.com

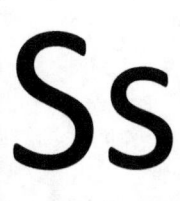

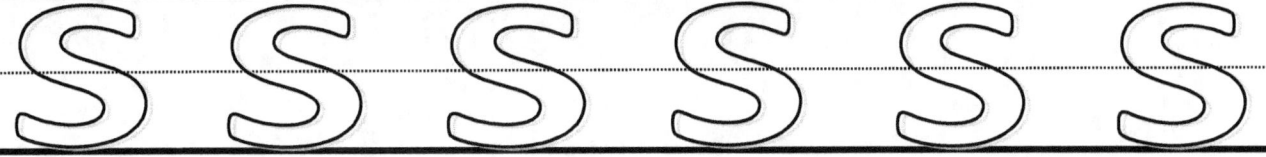
Name

Use a pencil or crayon to trace the big "S's" and little "s's" inside the lines.

S S S S S S S

s s s s s s s

Color and cut out the big "S" and little "s" at the bottom of the page, then match and paste in the box.

S s

s q S R

www.SpongyLittleMinds.com

Ss

_____
Name

Trace and follow the arrows. Then write your own big "S's" and little "s's" the same way.

Find and put an X on little "s" and big "S".

s r q s r s q s

S R S R Q R S R

www.SpongyLittleMinds.com

_____
Name

Trace and follow the arrows. Then write your own big "S's" and little "s's" the same way.

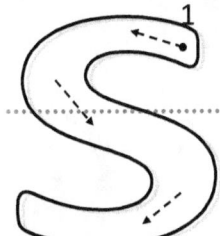

See if you can find and circle the big "S's" and little "s's" in these words. Parent note: Do not worry about the sounds of the words or what they say, this is more like a game for your child.

Samson	rhinoceros	seashell	Mt. Sinai
Revelation	Savior	sin	sheep
salvation	rain	Stephen	river
sunshine	scorpion	rest	seed
Samuel	self-control	Passover	Sarah

www.SpongyLittleMinds.com

_____
Name

Trace and follow the arrows. Then write your own big "S's" and little "s's" the same way.

Using a crayon, find big "S" and little "s", draw a line to connect them. Use a different color to connect big "R" and little "r", and still another color to connect big "Q" and little "q".

S   r
R   s
Q   q

www.SpongyLittleMinds.com

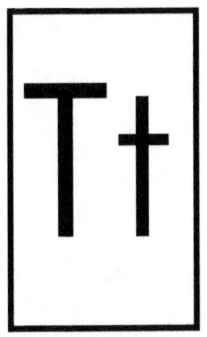

_____ Name

Use a pencil or crayon to trace the big "T's" and little "t's" inside the lines.

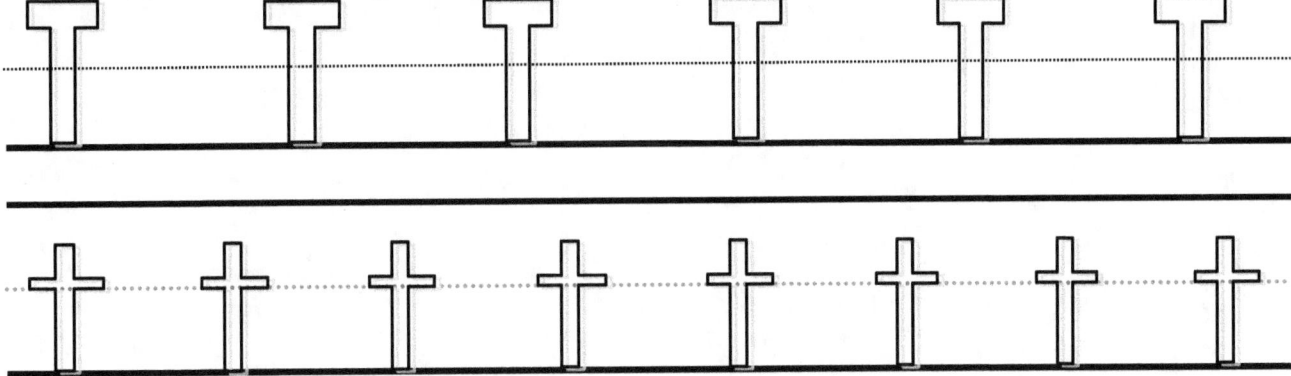

Color and cut out the big "T" and little "t" at the bottom of the page, then match and paste in the box.

www.SpongyLittleMinds.com

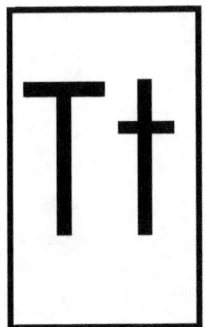

Name _____

Trace and follow the arrows. Then write your own big "T's" and little "t's" the same way.

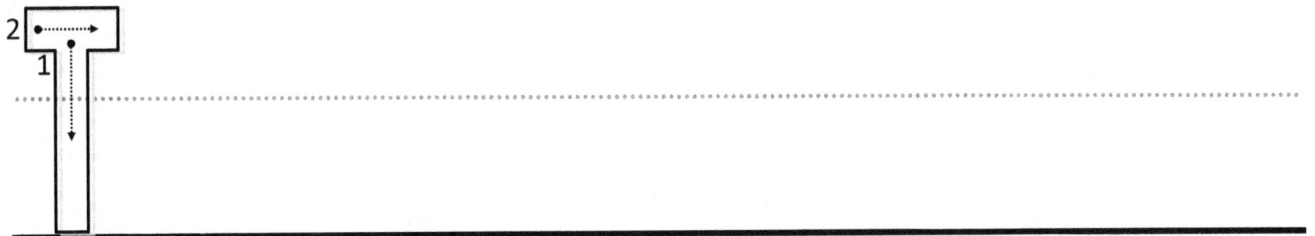

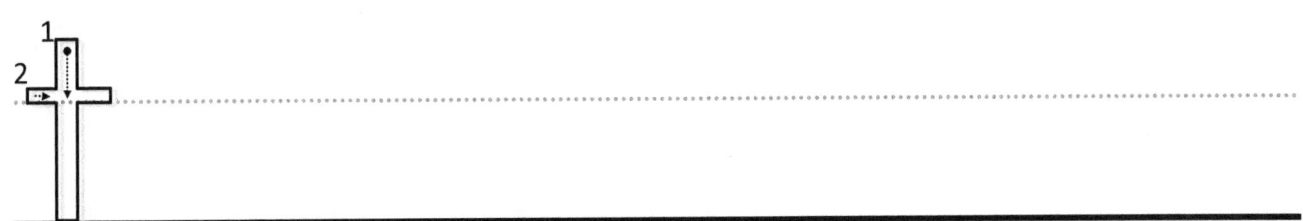

Find and put an X on little "t" and big "T".

s t t s t s t s
T R S T T R S T

www.SpongyLittleMinds.com

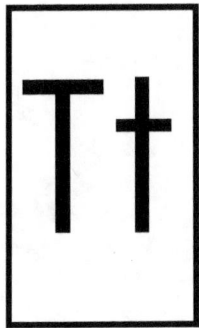

_____
Name

Trace and follow the arrows. Then write your own big "T's" and little "t's" the same way.

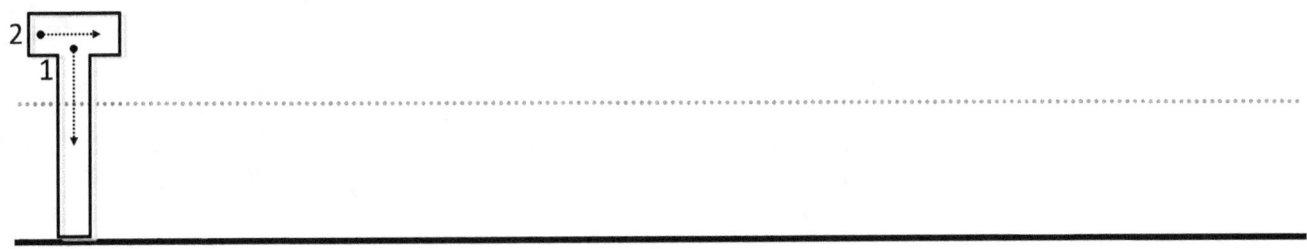

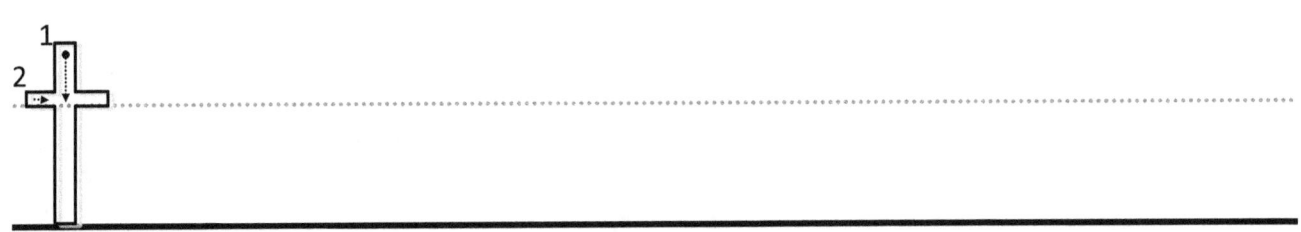

See if you can find and circle the big "T's" and little "t's" in these words. Parent note: Do not worry about the sounds of the words or what they say, this is more like a game for your child.

Samson	teacher	Thessalonians	Tina
Timothy	Savior	turtle	sheep
salvation	truth	typhoon	trinity
table	scorpion	rest	seed
tyranny	Tar shish	task	Tasha

www.SpongyLittleMinds.com

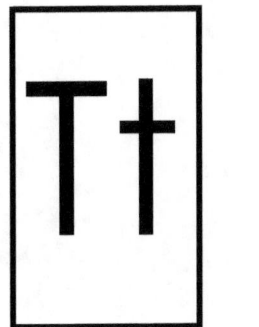

_____
Name

Trace and follow the arrows. Then write your own big "T's" and little "t's" the same way.

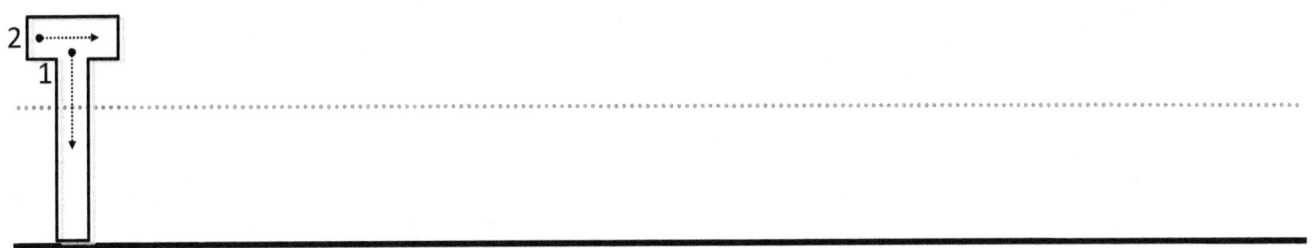

Using a crayon, find big "T" and little "t", draw a line to pair them up. Use a different color to pair up big "S" and little "s", and still another color to pair up big "R" and little "r".

www.SpongyLittleMinds.com

_____
Name

Use a pencil or crayon to trace the big "U's" and little "u's" inside the lines.

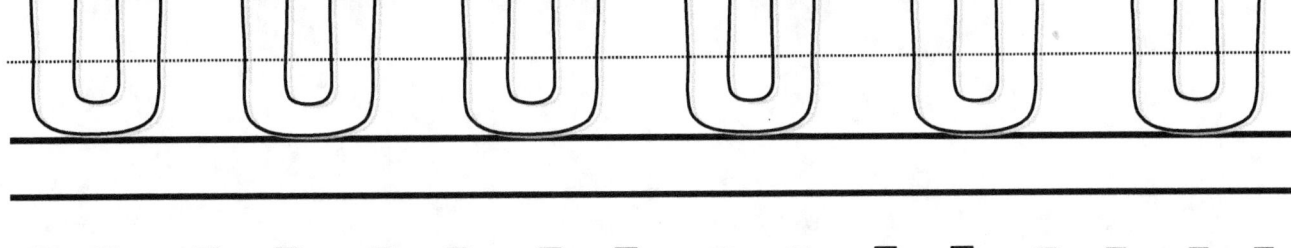

Color and cut out the big "U" and little "u" at the bottom of the page, then match and paste in the box.

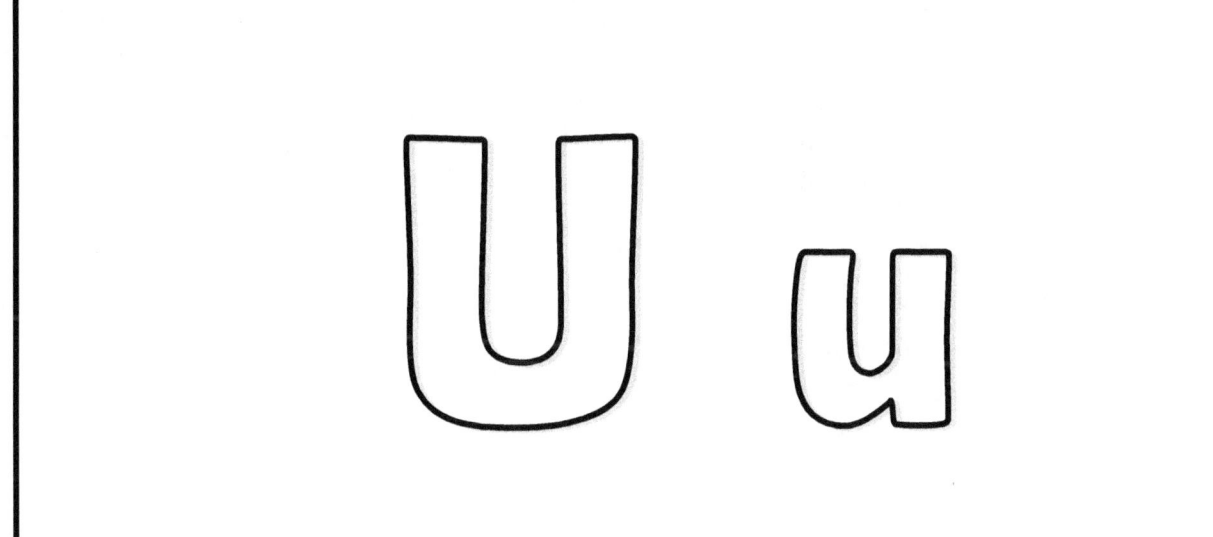

www.SpongyLittleMinds.com

_____
Name

Trace and follow the arrows. Then write your own big "U's" and little "u's" the same way.

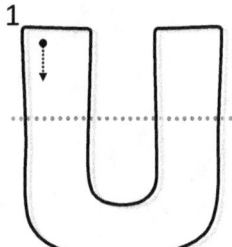

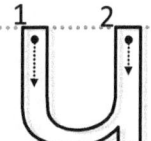

Find and put an X on little "u" and big "U".

u t s u t u t u
TUSUTUUT

www.SpongyLittleMinds.com

_____
Name

Trace and follow the arrows. Then write your own big "U's" and little "u's" the same way.

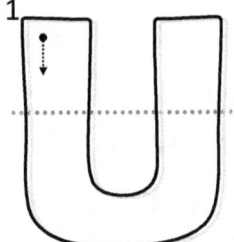

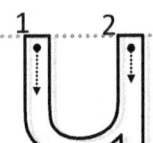

See if you can find and circle the big "U's" and little "u's" in these words. Parent note: Do not worry about the sounds of the words or what they say, this is more like a game for your child.

unbelief	teacher	Uncle	Tina
unclean	unity	turtle	umbrella
salvation	truth	universe	trinity
table	utterly	ukulele	uniform
Urim	urchin	task	Tasha

www.SpongyLittleMinds.com

_____
Name

Trace and follow the arrows. Then write your own big "U's" and little "u's" the same way.

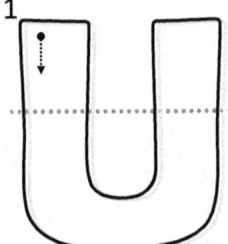

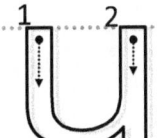

Using a crayon, find big "U" and little "u", draw a line to pair them up. Use a different color to pair up big "T" and little "t", and still another color to pair up big "S" and little "s".

T   u
S   s
U   t

www.SpongyLittleMinds.com

_____
Name

Use a pencil or crayon to trace the big "V's" and little "v's" inside the lines.

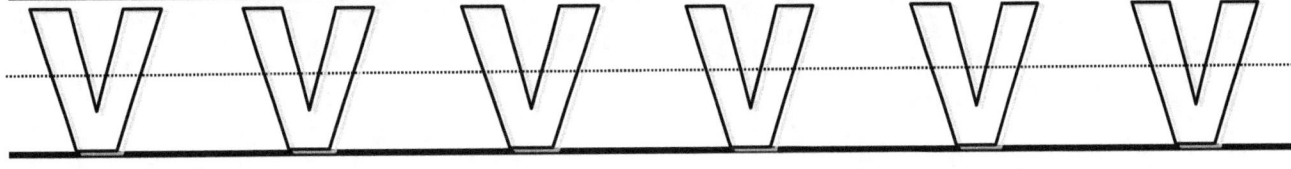

Color and cut out the big "V" and little "v" at the bottom of the page, then match and paste in the box.

www.SpongyLittleMinds.com

_____
Name

Trace and follow the arrows. Then write your own big "V's" and little "v's" the same way.

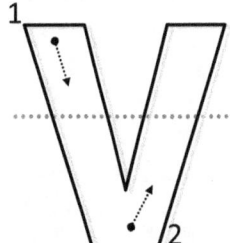

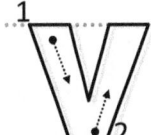

Find and put an X on little "v" and big "V".

v t v u v u v u

V U V U V U U V

www.SpongyLittleMinds.com

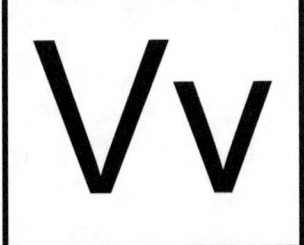

_____
Name

Trace and follow the arrows. Then write your own big "V's" and little "v's" the same way.

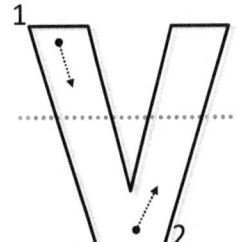

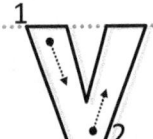

See if you can find and circle the big "V's" and little "v's" in these words. Parent note: Do not worry about the sounds of the words or what they say, this is more like a game for your child.

Vashti	vine	violet	valiant
unclean	unity	victory	umbrella
salvation	Venus	universe	violin
vole	utterly	ukulele	uniform
vulture	vision	veil	vow

www.SpongyLittleMinds.com

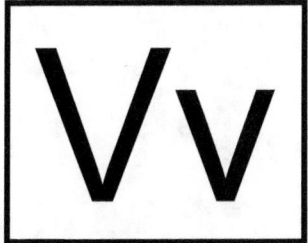

_____
Name

Trace and follow the arrows. Then write your own big "V's" and little "v's" the same way.

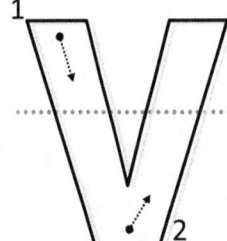

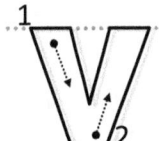

Using a crayon, find big "V" and little "v", draw a line to pair them up. Use a different color to pair up big "U" and little "u", and still another color to pair up big "T" and little "t".

www.SpongyLittleMinds.com

_____
Name

Use a pencil or crayon to trace the big "W's" and little "w's" inside the lines.

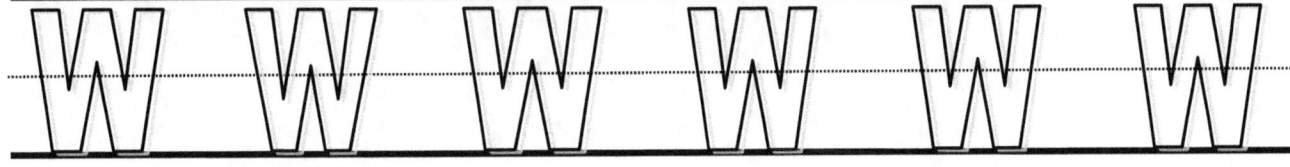

Color and cut out the big "W" and little "w" at the bottom of the page, then match and paste in the box.

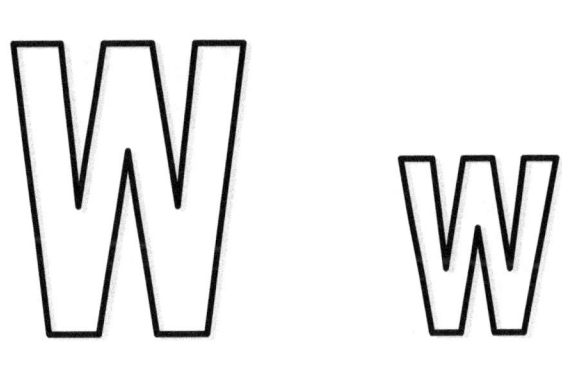

www.SpongyLittleMinds.com

_____
Name

Trace and follow the arrows. Then write your own big "W's" and little "w's" the same way.

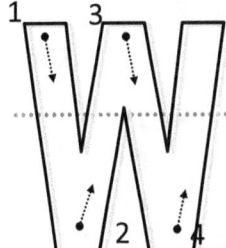

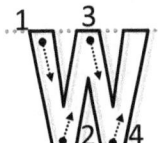

Find and put an X on little "w" and big "W".

www.SpongyLittleMinds.com

_____
Name

Trace and follow the arrows. Then write your own big "W's" and little "w's" the same way.

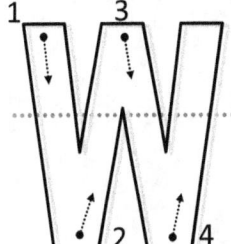

See if you can find and circle the big "W's" and little "w's" in these words. Parent note: Do not worry about the sounds of the words or what they say, this is more like a game for your child.

wisdom	vine	worthy	valiant
unclean	worship	victory	West
whale	vain	wages	violin
vacuum	Wormwood	war	winter
world	vision	wolf	vow

www.SpongyLittleMinds.com

_____
Name

Trace and follow the arrows. Then write your own big "W's" and little "w's" the same way.

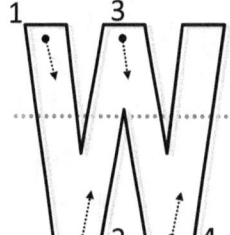

Using a crayon, find big "W" and little "w", draw a line to pair them up. Use a different color to pair up big "V" and little "v", and still another color to pair up big "U" and little "u".

www.SpongyLittleMinds.com

_____
Name

Use a pencil or crayon to trace the big "X's" and little "x's" inside the lines.

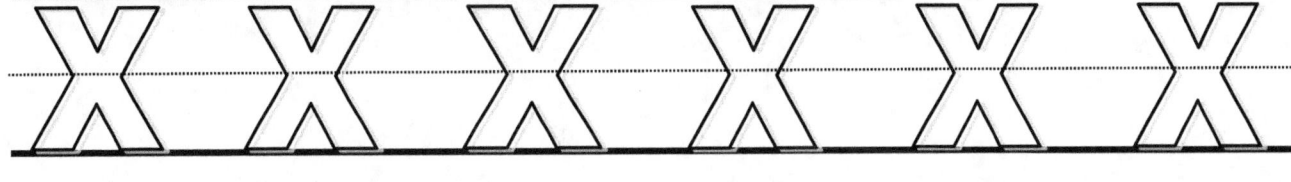

Color and cut out the big "X" and little "x" at the bottom of the page, then match and paste in the box.

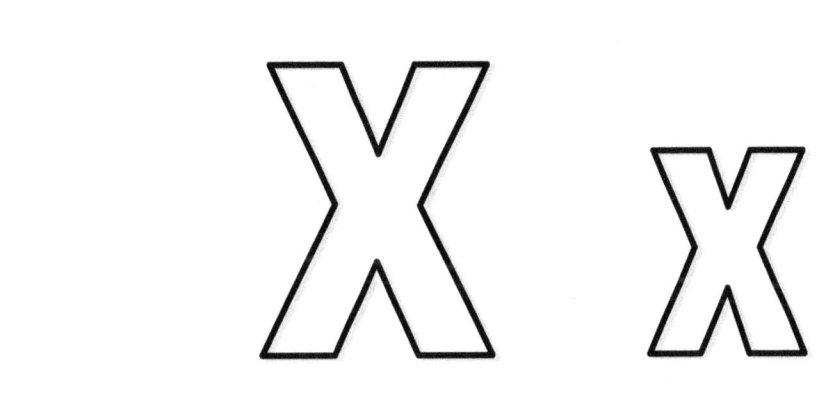

www.SpongyLittleMinds.com

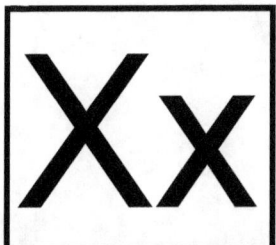

_____
Name

Trace and follow the arrows. Then write your own big "X's" and little "x's" the same way.

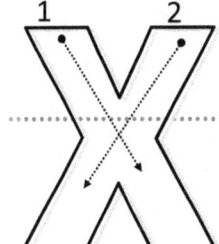

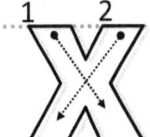

Find and put an X on little "x" and big "X".

www.SpongyLittleMinds.com

_____
Name

Trace and follow the arrows. Then write your own big "X's" and little "x's" the same way.

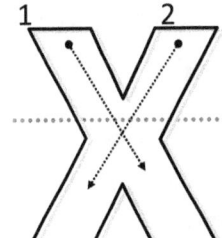

See if you can find and circle the big "X's" and little "x's" in these words. Parent note: Do not worry about the sounds of the words or what they say, this is more like a game for your child.

xylophone	vine	worthy	flax
axe	toxic	phlox	West
whale	exhale	wages	relax
vacuum	onyx	xerox	tax
Xerxes	vision	x-ray	vow

www.SpongyLittleMinds.com

_____
Name

Trace and follow the arrows. Then write your own big "X's" and little "x's" the same way.

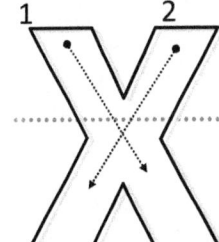

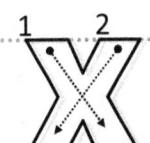

Using a crayon, find big "X" and little "X", draw a line to pair them up. Use a different color to pair up big "W" and little "w", and still another color to pair up big "V" and little "v".

www.SpongyLittleMinds.com

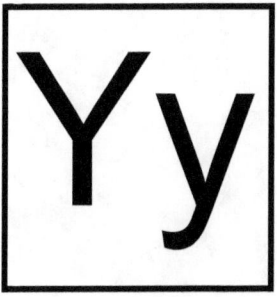

_____ Name

Use a pencil or crayon to trace the big "Y's" and little "y's" inside the lines.

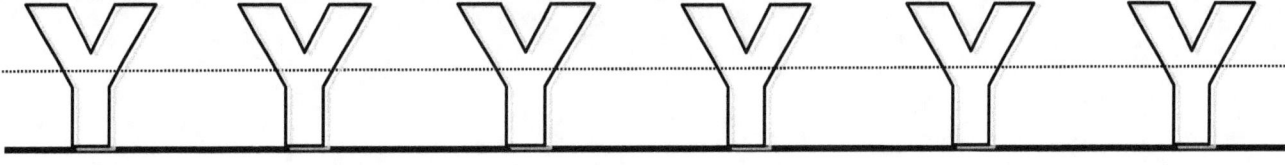

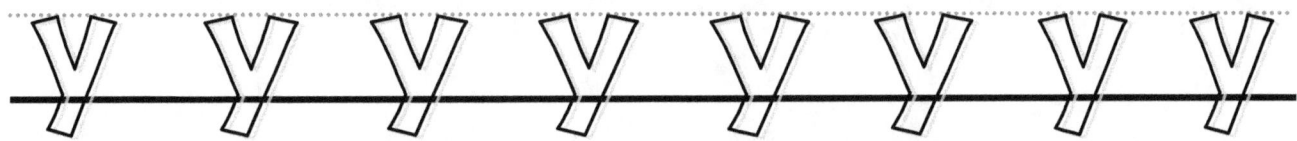

Color and cut out the big "Y" and little "y" at the bottom of the page, then match and paste in the box.

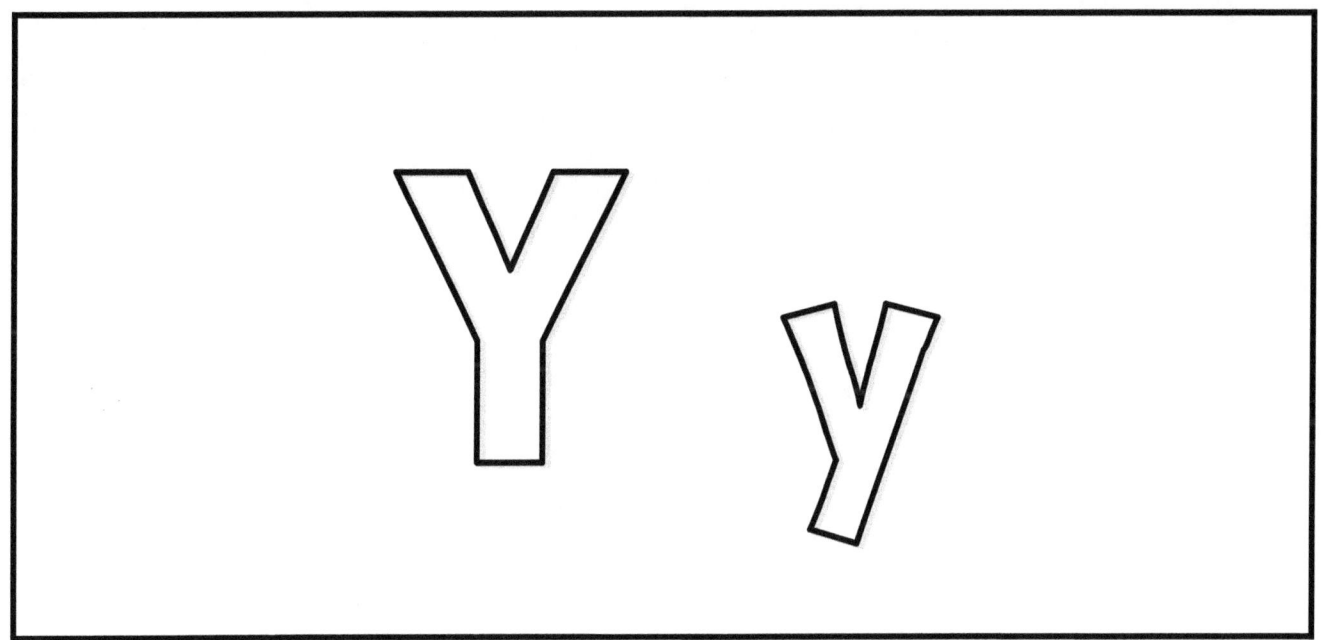

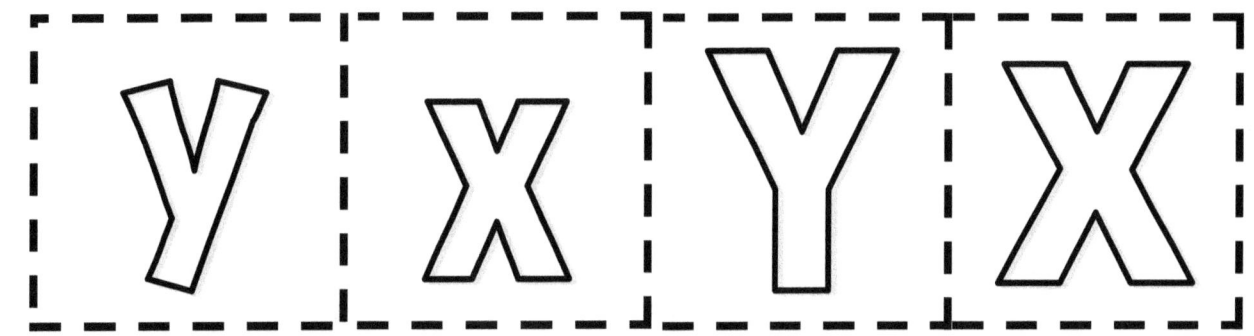

www.SpongyLittleMinds.com

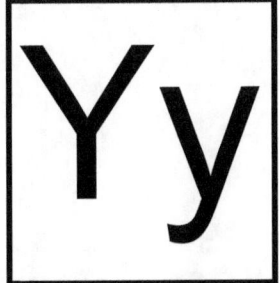

_____
Name

Trace and follow the arrows. Then write your own big "Y's" and little "y's" the same way.

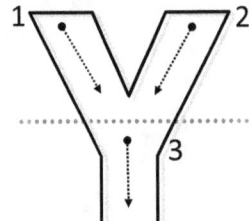

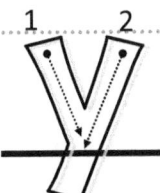

Find and put an X on little "y" and big "Y".

www.SpongyLittleMinds.com

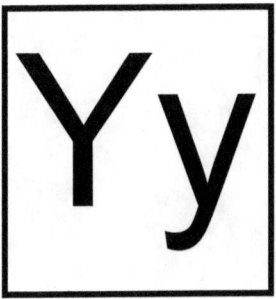

_____
Name

Trace and follow the arrows. Then write your own big "Y's" and little "y's" the same way.

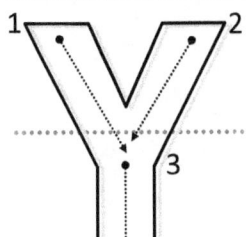

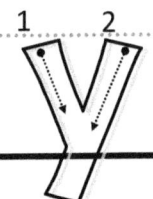

See if you can find and circle the big "Y's" and little "y's" in these words. Parent note: Do not worry about the sounds of the words or what they say, this is more like a game for your child.

wisdom	yawn	worthy	destiny
yellow	worship	victory	West
yield	vain	yoke	day
vacuum	Yankee	war	young
yak	vision	Yale	vow

www.SpongyLittleMinds.com

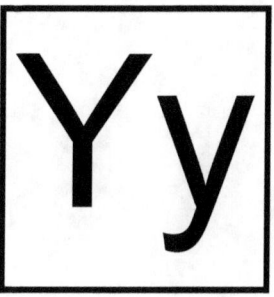

_____
Name

Trace and follow the arrows. Then write your own big "Y's" and little "y's" the same way.

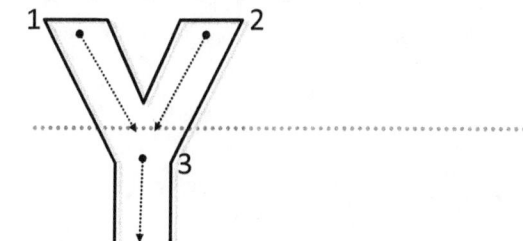

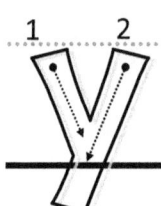

Using a crayon, find big "Y" and little "y", draw a line to pair them up. Use a different color to pair up big "X" and little "x", and still another color to pair up big "W" and little "w".

www.SpongyLittleMinds.com

_____
Name

Use a pencil or crayon to trace the big "Z's" and little "z's" inside the lines.

Z Z Z Z Z Z Z Z

z z z z z z z z

Color and cut out the big "Z" and little "z" at the bottom of the page, then match and paste in the box.

Z z

Z X Y Z

www.SpongyLittleMinds.com

Zz

_____
Name

Trace and follow the arrows. Then write your own big "Z's" and little "z's" the same way.

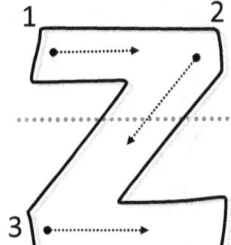

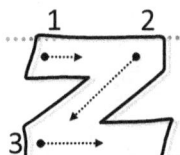

Find and put an X on little "z" and big "Z".

z y x z y z y z

Y Z X W Z X Z

www.SpongyLittleMinds.com

_____
Name

Trace and follow the arrows. Then write your own big "Z's" and little "z's" the same way.

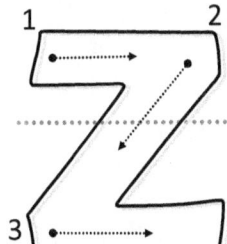

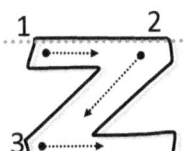

See if you can find and circle the big "Z's" and little "z's" in these words. Parent note: Do not worry about the sounds of the words or what they say, this is more like a game for your child.

zebra	yawn	zilch	valiant
yellow	Zane	victory	zoo
zipper	vain	zigzag	violin
vacuum	zeal	war	Zion
Zipporah	vision	zink	vow

www.SpongyLittleMinds.com

_____
Name

Trace and follow the arrows. Then write your own big "Z's" and little "z's" the same way.

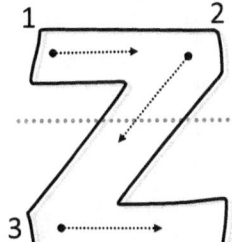

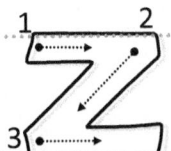

Using a crayon, find big "Z" and little "z", draw a line to pair them up. Use a different color to pair up big "Y" and little "y", and still another color to pair up big "X" and little "x".

www.SpongyLittleMinds.com

Congratulations!

Write your name below.

_____

you have successfully completed your letter workbook. Keep up the good work!

You have a very spongy little mind.

Great Job!

Have a blast coloring this page! And be sure to practice the letters everyday.

www.ingramcontent.com/pod-product-compliance
Lightning Source LLC
LaVergne TN
LVHW081356060426
835510LV00016B/1868

9 780692 754894